HITLER'S AMERICAN MODEL

HITLER'S AMERICAN MODEL

THE UNITED STATES AND THE MAKING OF NAZI RACE LAW

James Q. Whitman

PRINCETON UNIVERSITY PRESS

Princeton and Oxford

Copyright © 2017 by Princeton University Press

Published by Princeton University Press,
41 William Street, Princeton, New Jersey 08540
In the United Kingdom: Princeton University Press,
6 Oxford Street, Woodstock, Oxfordshire OX20 1TR

press.princeton.edu

Cover design by Faceout Studio, Charles Brock

ISBN 978-0-691-17242-2

Library of Congress Control Number: 2016960238

British Library Cataloging-in-Publication Data is available

This book has been composed in Futura Std and Sabon Next LT Pro

Printed on acid-free paper. ∞

Printed in the United States of America

1 3 5 7 9 10 8 6 4 2

FOR THE GHOST OF
LOUIS B. BRODSKY

CONTENTS

A NOTE ON TRANSLATIONS

Translations of German texts are all my own, unless otherwise noted. I have done my best to render the originals into idiomatic English without distorting their sense. Readers can consult the key passages in the original at http://press.princeton.edu/titles/10925.html.

One German text is especially important: the transcript of the June 5, 1934, meeting discussed in detail in Chapter 2. That transcript appears in a German multivolume series publishing materials on the drafting history of German criminal law and criminal procedure: Jürgen Regge and Werner Schubert, eds., *Quellen zur Reform des Straf-und Strafprozeßrechts* (Berlin: De Gruyter, 1988–). The relevant volume (vol. 2:2, pt. 2) includes two versions of the transcript, one full and unedited, and the other subsequently edited down in consultation with the participants. The series is available at major American law libraries. Since the transcript is a stenographic record of a daylong meeting, it is too lengthy to be reproduced in full.

HITLER'S AMERICAN MODEL

INTRODUCTION

This jurisprudence would suit us perfectly, with a single exception.
Over there they have in mind, practically speaking, only coloreds and
half-coloreds, which includes mestizos and mulattoes; but the Jews,
who are also of interest to us, are not reckoned among the coloreds.

—Roland Freisler, *June 5, 1934*

On June 5, 1934, about a year and a half after Adolf Hitler became
Chancellor of the Reich, the leading lawyers of Nazi Germany
gathered at a meeting to plan what would become the Nuremberg
Laws, the notorious anti-Jewish legislation of the Nazi race regime.
The meeting was chaired by Franz Gürtner, the Reich Minister of
Justice, and attended by officials who in the coming years would
play central roles in the persecution of Germany's Jews. Among
those present was Bernhard Lösener, one of the principal draftsmen of the Nuremberg Laws; and the terrifying Roland Freisler,
later President of the Nazi People's Court and a man whose name
has endured as a byword for twentieth-century judicial savagery.

The meeting was an important one, and a stenographer was present to record a verbatim transcript, to be preserved by the ever-
diligent Nazi bureaucracy as a record of a crucial moment in the
creation of the new race regime. That transcript reveals the startling fact that is my point of departure in this study: the meeting
involved detailed and lengthy discussions of the law of the United

States. In the opening minutes, Justice Minister Gürtner presented a memo on American race law, which had been carefully prepared by the officials of the ministry for purposes of the gathering; and the participants returned repeatedly to the American models of racist legislation in the course of their discussions. It is particularly startling to discover that the most radical Nazis present were the most ardent champions of the lessons that American approaches held for Germany. Nor, as we shall see, is this transcript the only record of Nazi engagement with American race law. In the late 1920s and early 1930s many Nazis, including not least Hitler himself, took a serious interest in the racist legislation of the United States. Indeed in *Mein Kampf* Hitler praised America as nothing less than "the one state" that had made progress toward the creation of a healthy racist order of the kind the Nuremberg Laws were intended to establish.

My purpose is to chronicle this neglected history of Nazi efforts to mine American race law for inspiration during the making of the Nuremberg Laws, and to ask what it tells us about Nazi Germany, about the modern history of racism, and especially about America.

✦

The Nazi persecution of the Jews and others, culminating in the Holocaust, counts for all of us as the supremely horrible crime of the twentieth century, and the notion that Nazi policy makers might have been in some way inspired by American models may seem a bit too awful to contemplate. It may also seem implausible: we all think of America, whatever its undeniable faults, as the home of liberty and democracy—as a country that put all of its might into the battle against fascism and Nazism that was finally won in 1945. Of course we also all know that America was home to its own racism in the era of the Nazi ascent to power, particularly in the Jim Crow South. In the 1930s Nazi Germany and the American South had the look, in the words of two southern historians, of a "mirror image":[1] these were two unapologetically racist regimes, unmatched in their pitilessness. In the early 1930s the Jews of Germany were hounded, beaten, and sometimes murdered, by mobs and by the state alike. In the same years the blacks of the American South were hounded, beaten, and sometimes murdered as well.[2]

Nevertheless the idea that American law might have exerted any sort of direct influence on the Nazi program of racial persecution and oppression is hard to digest. Whatever similarities there may have been among the racist regimes of the 1930s, however foul the history of American racism may be, we are accustomed to thinking of Nazism as an ultimately unparalleled horror. The crimes of the Nazis are the *nefandum*, the unspeakable descent into what we often call "radical evil." No one wants to imagine that America provided any measure of inspiration for Hitler. In any case, it may seem inherently improbable that Nazis would have felt the need to look to any other country for lessons in racism—perhaps least of all to the United States, which is, after all, whatever its failings, the home of a great constitutional tradition founded in liberty.

And virtually no one has suggested otherwise, with the notable exception of a shrewd paragraph in Mark Mazower's 2008 book *Hitler's Empire*.[3] Other scholars have insisted on what most of us must think of as the obvious truth: There was of course no direct American influence on Nazi race law, or at least no meaningful influence. Whatever similarities there may have been, the Nazis were the authors of their own monstrous work; certainly America had nothing to teach Hitler. The person who has given the question the most sustained attention is a German lawyer named Andreas Rethmeier, who wrote a 1995 dissertation on the Nuremberg Laws that included an examination of some of the many Nazi references to American law.[4] After reviewing his data Rethmeier arrived at a disconcerting verdict: America was, for the Nazis, the "classic example" of a country with racist legislation.[5] Nevertheless, he insisted forcefully that the idea of American influence on the Nuremberg Laws was "not just off-base, but plain wrong." After all, he argued, the Americans classified Jews as "Caucasian," a gross error from the Nazi point of view.[6]

Others have come to similar conclusions. "[T]he few and fleeting references by Nazi polemicists and 'jurists' to Jim Crow laws," writes the American legal historian Richard Bernstein, for example, "were, as far as I can tell, simply attempts to cite vaguely relevant precedents for home-grown statutes and policies to deflect criticism, not actual sources of intellectual influence."[7] "[T]he segregation law of the states," declares similarly Marcus Hanke of the University of Salzburg, "has not been of any important influence."[8] Most recently, Jens-Uwe Guettel has written, in a 2012 book, of what he calls the "astonishing insignificance of American segregation laws" for Nazi policies. The Nazis, Guettel insists, regarded America as hopelessly mired in an outdated liberal outlook.[9] There was nothing that deserves the name of influence. All of these scholars are perfectly aware that the Nazis had things to say about American law. But their reassuring consensus is that the Nazis said them merely in order to claim a specious parallel to their racist programs in the face of international condemnation.[10] The Nazis were interested in taunting America, not learning from it.

The sources, read soberly, paint a different picture. Awful it may be to contemplate, but the reality is that the Nazis took a sustained, significant, and sometimes even eager interest in the American example in race law. They most certainly *were* interested in learning from America. In fact, as we shall see, it was the most radical Nazis who pushed most energetically for the exploitation of American models. Nazi references to American law were neither few nor fleeting, and Nazi discussions took place in policy-making contexts that had nothing to do with producing international propaganda on behalf of the regime. Nor, importantly, was it only, or even primarily, the Jim Crow South that attracted Nazi lawyers. In the early 1930s the Nazis drew on a range of American examples, both federal and state. Their America was not just the South; it was a racist America writ much larger. Moreover, the ironic truth is that when Nazis rejected the American example, it was sometimes because they thought that American practices were overly harsh: for Nazis of the early 1930s, even radical ones, American race law sometimes looked *too* racist.

Be it emphasized immediately that there was certainly never anything remotely like unmixed admiration for America among the Nazis, who aggressively rejected the liberal and democratic commitments of American government. The Nazis were never interested in simply replicating the United States in Central Europe. Nevertheless Nazi lawyers regarded America, not without reason, as the innovative world leader in the creation of racist law; and while they saw much to deplore, they also saw much to emulate. It is even possible, indeed likely, that the Nuremberg Laws themselves reflect direct American influence.

★

The proposition that the Nazis drew inspiration from American race law in creating their own program of racist persecution is sure to seem distressing; no one wants the taint of an association with the crimes of Nazism. But in the end it should really come as no great surprise to attentive readers of Nazi history. In recent years historians have published considerable evidence of Nazi interest in, and even admiration for, a range of American practices, programs, and achievements. Especially in the early years of the regime, the Nazis did not by any means regard the United States as a clear ideological enemy.

In part, the Nazis looked to America for the same more or less innocent reasons others did all around the globe. The United States is powerful, wealthy, and creative, and even its most visceral enemies have found things to admire about it. During the century or so since 1918 the glamour of America has proven particularly hard to resist. As interwar German racists observed, the United States had emerged after World War I as "the premier power in the world";[11] it is hardly a surprise that the Nazis, like others, looked for what lessons the global powerhouse might have to teach, even as they also derided the liberal and democratic commitments of American society. Like others, the Nazis were impressed by the vigor of American industrial innovativeness and the vibrancy of Hollywood culture (though their taste for American culture was heavily qualified by their disgust for the "Negro music" of Jazz).[12] Hitler in particular voiced his admiration, in *Mein Kampf*, for the "wealth of inventions" generated by the United States.[13] None of this was peculiar to Nazi Germany.[14]

But historians have shown that there were also things about America that appealed to more distinctively Nazi views and goals. Some of this involved the American politics of the early 1930s. We have long known the strange fact that the Nazis frequently praised Franklin Roosevelt and New Deal government in the early 1930s. FDR received distinctly favorable treatment in the Nazi press until at least 1936 or 1937, lauded as a man who had seized "dictatorial powers" and embarked upon "bold experiments" in the spirit of the Führer.[15] Similar things were said more broadly about what was sometimes labeled in the 1930s "the fascist New Deal."[16] The glossy *Berlin Illustrated Magazine*, seized from its Jewish publisher and converted into a kind of Nazi *Life* magazine, ran heroic photo spreads on Roosevelt,[17] while Nazi rags like *Will and Power*, the newsletter of the Hitler Youth, described him as a "revolutionary" who might fail only because he lacked "a disciplined Party army like our Führer."[18] Meanwhile Roosevelt, for his part, though he was certainly troubled by the persecution of the German Jews and had harsh words for "dictators," cautiously refrained from singling out Hitler until 1937 or even 1939.[19] There were certainly not deep ties of friendship between the two governments in the early 1930s, but the pall of unconditional hostility had not yet clearly fallen over US–German relations either. In this connection it is worth emphasizing, as the political scientist Ira Katznelson has recently done, that the New Deal depended heavily on the political support of the segregationist South.[20] The relationship between the northern and southern Democrats was particularly cozy during the early 1930s, a period when, as we shall see, Nazi observers were particularly hopeful that they could "reach out the hand of friendship" to the United States on the basis of a shared commitment to white supremacy.[21]

To be sure, there are ways of minimizing the significance of the favorable press given to New Deal America in Nazi Germany. Nobody would suggest that Hitler was inspired by the example of FDR to become a dictator; and in any case the reality is that the American president was a committed democrat, who preserved American constitutional government at a time when it was under ominous stress.[22] If the United States and Germany, both confronting the immense challenges of the Great Depression, found themselves resorting to similar "bold experiments," that does not make them intimate bedfellows.[23] And whatever the Nazis may have thought about southern racism, southern whites themselves did not generally become supporters of Hitler.[24] If the Nazis regarded New Deal America as a potential comrade in arms, that does not necessarily tell us much about what kind of a country America really was.

But—and here recent scholarship on German–American relations becomes more troubling—historians have also tracked down

American influence on some of the most unambiguously criminal Nazi programs—in particular on Nazi eugenics and the murderous Nazi conquests in Eastern Europe.

Begin with eugenics. A ruthless program of eugenics, designed to build a "healthy" society, free of hereditary defects, was central to Nazi ambitions in the 1930s. Soon after taking power, the regime passed a Law to Prevent the Birth of the Offspring with Hereditary Defects, and by the end of the decade a program of systematic euthanasia that prefigured the Holocaust, including the use of gassing, was under way.[25] We now know that in the background of this horror lay a sustained engagement with America's eugenics movement. In his 1994 book *The Nazi Connection: Eugenics, American Racism, and German National Socialism*, historian Stefan Kühl created a sensation by demonstrating that there was an active back-and-forth traffic between American and Nazi eugenicists until the late 1930s, indeed that Nazis even looked to the United States as a "model."[26] During the interwar period the United States was not just a global leader in assembly-line manufacturing and Hollywood popular culture. It was also a global leader in "scientific" eugenics, led by figures like the historian Lothrop Stoddard and the lawyer Madison Grant, author of the 1916 racist best-seller *The Passing of the Great Race; or, The Racial Basis of European History*. These were men who promoted the sterilization of the mentally defective and the exclusion of immigrants who were supposedly genetically inferior. Their teachings filtered into immigration law not only in the United States but also in other Anglophone countries: Britain, Australia, Canada, and New Zealand all began to screen immigrants for their hereditary fitness.[27] Kühl demonstrated that the impact of American eugenics was also strongly felt in Nazi Germany, where the works of Grant, Stoddard, and other American eugenicists were standard citations.

To be sure, there are, here again, ways we may try to minimize the significance of the eugenics story. American eugenicists, repellant though they were, did not advocate mass euthanasia, and the period when the Nazis moved in their most radically murderous direction, at the very end of the 1930s, was also the period when their direct links with American eugenics frayed. In any case, eugenics, which was widely regarded as quite respectable at the time, was an international movement, whose reach extended beyond the borders of both the United States and Nazi Germany. The global history of eugenics cannot be told as an exclusively German–American tale. But the story of Nazi interest in the American example does not end with the eugenics of the early 1930s; historians have carried it into the nightmare years of the Holocaust in the early 1940s as well.

It is here that some of the most unsettling evidence has been assembled, as historians have shown that Nazi expansion eastward was accompanied by invocations of the American conquest of the West, with its accompanying wars on Native Americans. This tale, by contrast with the tale of eugenics, is a much more exclusively German–American one. The Nazis were consumed by the felt imperative to acquire *Lebensraum*, "living space," for an expanding Germany that would engulf the territories to its east, and "[f]or generations of German imperialists, and for Hitler himself, the exemplary land empire was the United States of America."[28] In Nazi eyes, the United States ranked alongside the British, "to be respected as racial kindred and builders of a great empire":[29] both were "Nordic" polities that had undertaken epic programs of conquest.

Indeed as early as 1928 Hitler was speechifying admiringly about the way Americans had "gunned down the millions of Redskins to a few hundred thousand, and now keep the modest remnant under observation in a cage";[30] and during the years of genocide in the early 1940s Nazi leaders made repeated reference to the American conquest of the West when speaking of their own murderous conquests to their east.[31] Historians have compiled many quotes, from Hitler and others, comparing Germany's conquests, and its program of extermination, with America's winning of the West. They are quotes that make for chilling reading, and there are historians who try to deny their significance.[32] But the majority of scholars find the evidence too weighty to reject: "The United States policy of westward expansion," as Norman Rich forcefully concludes, for example, "in the course of which the white men ruthlessly thrust aside the 'inferior' indigenous populations, served as the model for Hitler's entire conception of *Lebensraum*."[33]

All of this adds up to a tale of considerable Nazi interest in what the example of the United States had to offer. It is a tale that has to be told cautiously. It is surely too much to call the United States "the" model for Nazi Germany without careful qualification; Nazi attitudes toward America were too ambivalent, and Nazi programs had too many indigenous sources. America, for its part, as we shall see, embodied too much of what the Nazis hated most, at least in its better moments. If the Nazis found precedents and parallels and inspirations in America, they nevertheless struck out on their own path. Still, what all this research unmistakably reveals is that the Nazis *did* find precedents and parallels and inspirations in the United States.

✶

It is against that background that I ask the reader to ponder the evidence that this book has to present. In the early 1930s, as the Nazis were crafting the program of racial persecution enshrined in the Nuremberg Laws, they took a great interest not only in the way Henry Ford built cars for the masses, not only in the way Hollywood built its own mass market, not only in FDR's style of government, not only in American eugenics, and not only in American westward expansion, but also in the lessons to be garnered from the techniques of American racist legislation and jurisprudence.

Scholars have failed to write this history for two reasons: they have been looking in the wrong place and have been employing the wrong interpretive tools. First and foremost, they have been looking in the wrong place. Scholars like Guettel and Hanke have addressed their question in unmistakably American terms. What Americans ask is whether "Jim Crow" had any influence on the Nazis; and by "Jim Crow" they mean segregation as it was practiced in the American South and fought over in the American civil rights era from the early 1950s into the mid-1960s—segregation in education, public transportation, housing, and the like. Looking for an influence of American segregation law on the Nazis, Guettel and Hanke conclude that there was little or none. Now, as we shall see, that conclusion is too hasty. The Nazis *did* know, and did care, about American segregation; and it is clear that some of them *were* intrigued by the possibility of bringing Jim Crow to Germany. As we shall see, important programmatic Nazi texts made a point of invoking the example of Jim Crow segregation, and there were leading Nazi lawyers who made serious proposals that something similar ought to be introduced into Germany.[34] But the principal difficulty with the conclusions of Guettel and Hanke is that they are answering the wrong question. Segregation is not what counts most.

Yes it is true that segregation in the style of the American South did not matter all that much to the Nazi regime—but that is for the simple reason that segregation was not all that central to the Nazi program. The Nuremberg Laws said nothing about segregation. Their concern, and the overwhelming concern of the Nazi regime of the early 1930s, lay in two other domains: first, citizenship, and second, sex and reproduction. The Nazis were committed to the proposition that "every state has the right to maintain its population pure and unmixed,"[35] safe from racial pollution. To that end they were determined to establish a citizenship regime that would be firmly founded on racial categories. They were further determined to prevent mixed marriages between Jews and "Aryans," and to criminalize extramarital sex between members of the two communities.[36]

In both respects they found, and welcomed, precedent and authority in American law, and by no means just in the law of the South. In the 1930s the United States, as the Nazis frequently noted, stood at the forefront of race-based lawmaking. American immigration and naturalization law, in the shape of a series of laws culminating in the Immigration Act of 1924, conditioned entry into the United States on race-based tables of "national origins." It was America's race-based immigration law that Hitler praised in *Mein Kampf*, in a passage that has been oddly neglected by American legal scholars; and leading Nazi legal thinkers did the same after him, repeatedly and volubly. The United States also stood at the forefront in the creation of forms of de jure and de facto second-class citizenship for blacks, Filipinos, Chinese, and others; this too was of great interest to the Nazis, engaged as they were in creating their own forms of second-class citizenship for Germany's Jews. As for race mixing between the sexes, the United States stood at the forefront there as well. America was a beacon of anti-miscegenation law, with thirty different state regimes—many of them outside the South, and all of them (as we shall see) carefully studied, catalogued, and debated by Nazi lawyers. There were no other models for miscegenation legislation that the Nazis could find in the world, a fact that Justice Minister Gürtner highlighted at the June 5, 1934, meeting with which I began. When it came to immigration, second-class citizenship, and miscegenation, America was indeed "the classic example" of a country with highly developed, and harsh, race law in the early 1930s, and Nazi lawyers made repeated reference to American models and precedents in the drafting process that led up to the Nuremberg Laws and continued in their subsequent interpretation and application. The tale is by no means one of "astonishing insignificance."

The scholars who dismiss the possibility of American influence on Nazi lawmaking have also used the wrong interpretive tools in making their case. Our literature has taken a crass interpretive tack: it has assumed that we can speak of "influence" only where we find direct and unmodified, even verbatim, imitation. That is the assumption behind Rethmeier's confident assertion that American race law could not have influenced the Nazis, since American law did not specifically target Jews. We find the same assumption in Hanke: Nazi law was different, Hanke declares, because the German laws of the early 1930s were "but one step on the stair to the gas chambers."[37] Unlike American segregation laws, which simply applied the principle of "separate but equal," German laws were part of a program of extermination. Now part of the problem with this argument, which Hanke is by no means alone in offering,[38] is that its historical premise is false: It is simply not the case that the drafters of the Nuremberg laws were already aiming at the annihilation of the Jews in 1935. The concern of early Nazi policy was to drive the Jewish population into exile, or at the very least to marginalize it within the borders of the Reich, and there were serious conflicts among Nazi policy makers about how to achieve even that goal.

But in any case, it is a major interpretive fallacy on the part of all these scholars to suppose that we cannot speak of "influence" unless Nazi laws were perfectly congruent with American ones. As we shall see, Nazi lawyers had no difficulty exploiting American law on race, even if it had nothing to say about Jews as such. In any case, influence in comparative law is rarely just about literal imitation. Influence is a complex business of translation, creative adaptation, selective borrowing, and invocation of authority. All borrowers engage in tinkering and retrofitting; that is as true of the Nazis as it is of any other regime. All borrowers start from foreign models and then reshape them to meet their own circumstances; that is true of vicious racist borrowers just as it is true of everyone else.

Influence does not come just through verbatim borrowing. It comes through inspiration and example, and the United States had much inspiration and example to offer Nazi lawyers in the early 1930s, the era of the making of the Nuremberg Laws.

★

None of this is entirely easy to talk about. There is more than one reason why it is hard to look coolly on the question of whether the racist program of the Nazis was influenced by, or even paralleled by, what went on in other Western regimes—just as it is hard to admit the continuities between Nazism and the postwar European orders that replaced it. No one wants to be perceived as relativizing Nazi crimes. Germans in particular are generally understandably reluctant to engage in discussions that might smack of apologetics. Contemporary Germany rests on the moral foundation not only of the repudiation of Nazism, but also of the refusal to deny German responsibility for what happened under Hitler. Alluding to foreign influences remains largely out of bounds in Germany for that reason. Conversely no non-Germans want their country to be accused of any part in the genesis of Nazism. It is hard to overcome our sense that if we influenced Nazism we have polluted ourselves in ways that can never be cleansed. On the deepest level it is perhaps the case that we feel, throughout the Western world, a need to identify a true *nefandum*, an abyss of unexampled modern horror against which we can define ourselves, a wholly sui generis "radical evil"—a sort of dark star to steer by lest we lose our moral bearings.

But of course history does not make it that easy. Nazism was not simply a nightmarish parenthesis in history that bore no relationship to what came before and after; nor was it a completely unexampled racist horror. The Nazis were not simply demons who erupted out of some dark underworld to shatter what was good and just within the Western tradition, until they were put down by force of arms and the authentic humane and progressive values of Europe were restored. There were traditions of Western government within which they worked. There *were* continuities between Nazism and what came before and after. There *were* examples and inspirations on which the Nazis drew, and American race law was prominent among them.

None of this is to suggest that America was a Nazi country in the 1930s. Of course it was not, appalling as the law of the early and mid-twentieth century sometimes was. Of course the racist strains in American law coexisted and competed with some glorious humane and egalitarian strains. Of course thoughtful Americans reviled Nazism—though there were certainly some who fell for Hitler. The most famous of the lawyers among them was none other than Roscoe Pound, dean of the Harvard Law School, icon of advanced American legal thought, and a man who made little secret of his liking for Hitler in the 1930s.[39] Nazi lawyers for their part saw plenty of things to despise about America.

The point is not that the American and Nazi race regimes were the same, but that the Nazis found examples and precedents in the American legal race order that they valued highly, while simultaneously deploring, and puzzling over, the strength of the liberal countercurrent in a country with so much openly and unapologetically sanctioned racism. We can, and should, reject the sort of simpleminded anti-Americanism that blames the United States for all the evils of the world, or reduces America to nothing but its history of racism.[40] But there is no excuse for refusing to confront hard questions about our history, and about the history of American influence abroad. The American impact on the rest of the world is not limited to what makes Americans proudest about their country. It has also included aspects of the American past that we might prefer to forget.

We will not understand the history of National Socialist Germany, and more importantly the place of America in the larger history of world racism, unless we reckon with these facts. In the early 1930s, Nazi lawyers were engaged in creating a race law founded on anti-miscegenation law and race-based immigration, naturalization, and second-class citizenship law. They went looking for foreign models, and found them—in the United States of America.

CHAPTER 1

MAKING NAZI FLAGS
AND NAZI CITIZENS

The racially pure and still unmixed German has risen to become master
of the American continent, and he will remain the master, as long as he
does not fall victim to racial pollution.

—Adolf Hitler, *Mein Kampf* [1]

It is a curiosity to pick up the *New York Times* for September 16, 1935.
The lead article for that day reported on one of darkest moments in
the history of modern racism with the following headline, bolded
and in large type: **"REICH ADOPTS SWASTIKA AS NATION'S OFFICIAL
FLAG; Hitler's Reply to 'Insult.'"** [2] This was how the *Times*, like
most other American newspapers, reported on the promulgation,
one day earlier, of the most infamous piece of race legislation of the
interwar era, the Nazi Nuremberg Laws. Only below did the paper
add, in less aggressive type, a reference to what we remember, and
revile, about Nuremberg: "Anti-Jewish Laws Passed. Non-'Aryans'
Deprived of Citizenship and Right to Intermarry." These were the
measures we call "the Nuremberg Laws" today—the measures that
signaled the full-scale creation of a racist state in a Germany on the

road to the Holocaust. Why weren't the American headlines about *them*?

The answer has to do with the political genesis of the Nuremberg Laws—and it testifies to the complexity and ambivalence of relations between Nazi Germany and New Deal America in the early 1930s. There were moments, during the frightening and uncertain years from 1933 through 1936, when Nazi views of the United States were marked by anti-American resentment, hatred toward American Jews, and contempt for American constitutional values; but there were also moments when Nazis expressed hope for a future of good relations, and a belief in the kinship between the United States and Germany as countries both committed to maintaining "Nordic" supremacy.

The September 16 headlines in the American press had to do with a case of Nazi hatred toward American Jews. The Nuremberg Laws were indeed presented to the world as Nazi Germany's response to an "insult" to the swastika flag—and the "insult" in question had taken place in New York City. This was the so-called *Bremen* Incident of late July 1935, when rioters ripped the swastika from the German ocean liner SS *Bremen*. The rioters were arrested, only to be released by a Jewish magistrate named Louis Brodsky. It was in response to Brodsky's decision that the Nazis proclaimed the first of the three Nuremberg Laws, the Reich Flag Law, which enshrined the swastika as the exclusive national emblem of Germany. The triumph of the swastika in Germany can thus be said to symbolize, to some degree, the Nazi rejection of the liberal currents in American life, and of the place of Jews in American society.

But the other two Nuremberg Laws, those that deprived German Jews of the right of citizenship and the right to intermarry, the ones we remember today as the Nuremberg Laws, were different. They were not presented to the world as a rejection of America. In fact, when Hitler and Göring proclaimed the two new anti-Jewish laws at Nuremberg, they did so in speeches that were decorated with expressions of friendship toward the Roosevelt administration and the United States. And the uncomfortable truth, as we shall see in this chapter and the next, is that the two anti-Jewish measures that we call the Nuremberg Laws today, far from marking a clear German rejection of all American values, were crafted in an atmosphere of considerable interest in, and respect for, what the example of American race law had to offer; and they brought German law significantly closer in line with American law than had previously been the case.

THE FIRST NUREMBERG LAW:
OF NEW YORK JEWS AND NAZI FLAGS

When we speak of the "Nuremberg Laws" today, we (like Germans of the Nazi era)[3] refer only to the second and third out of three. These two were the Citizenship Law, which subjected Jews to a form of second-class citizenship, and the Blood Law, which criminalized marriage and sexual relations between Jews and "Aryans." Nevertheless, there were indeed three laws proclaimed at what the Nazis called the "Party Rally of Freedom" at Nuremberg on September 15, 1935; and in describing the politics of Nuremberg, and America's place in the Nazi legal mind of the early 1930s, it is appropriate to begin where the American newspapers began: with the first of them, the Reichsflaggengesetz, the Flag Law for the Reich, and the *Bremen* Incident that provoked it. The history of Flag Law is a window into the murky currents and countercurrents of hostility and tentative amity that characterized Nazi attitudes toward New Deal America in the early 1930s.

The *Bremen* Incident occurred in New York on July 26, 1935, during a hot summer marked by diplomatic clashes and street-level violence between New York opponents of Hitler and pro-German

demonstrators.[4] That evening some one thousand rioters, characterized by police reports as including "communist sympathizers,"
stormed the SS *Bremen*, one of the swiftest liners on the Atlantic and
the pride of German engineering.[5] Five of the demonstrators managed to clamber aboard, rip the swastika down, and toss it into the
Hudson River.

The five were arrested, but a diplomatic crisis broke out that
rumbled ominously for weeks. Immediately after the episode, the
US State Department made an effort to calm the situation, send-
ing a note expressing its regret that "the German national emblem
should . . . not have received the respect to which it is entitled";[6]
whatever hostility to Hitler there may have been in the streets of
New York, the administration was anxious, at this point in its history, to maintain good relations with the Third Reich.[7] Nevertheless
throughout the late summer the German press kept matters at a
boil. The crisis reached its climax on September 6, a week before
the opening ceremonies of the Nuremberg Rally, when Manhattan
Magistrate Louis Brodsky ordered the release of the five arrested
rioters, while delivering a fiery opinion denouncing Nazism in the
name of American freedoms.

Louis Brodsky, the New York Jew who triggered the Nuremberg
Laws, was an improbable protagonist in an international diplomatic
crisis. His career was shaped by both the opportunities and the obstacles that early twentieth-century America presented to Jews. He
graduated from NYU Law School in 1901, at the remarkable age
of seventeen.[8] But Jewish lawyers did not find it easy to make their
way into prestigious law firms or judgeships in early twentieth-
century America. It was certainly infinitely better to be a Jewish
lawyer in the United States than in Nazi Germany, but it was still
tough (as the Nazi literature of the early 1930s gleefully observed),[9]
and Brodsky took a different route. Through the sponsorship of

Tammany Hall, the corrupt New York Democratic political machine that often promoted the interests of ethnic minorities, he landed a patronage job as a magistrate in the Lower Manhattan detention center known as the Tombs.[10]

Tombs magistrates were very low-level judicial officers, responsible for bail hearings, night court, and the like,[11] and a whiff of corruption often clung to Tammany appointees. (Brodsky himself survived charges of corruption in 1931.)[12] Nevertheless Brodsky was a man who used his lowly patronage office to issue thunderous civil libertarian opinions of the kind more commonly authored by justices of the Supreme Court. Brodsky may have been a beneficiary of Tammany Hall politics, but he (like other Tammany figures)[13] was also an ardent champion of American constitutional rights. In 1931 he stirred up a scandal by permitting the distribution of pornographic novels.[14] In April 1935 he made headlines again when he released two nude dancers who had been arrested at a Greenwich Village club, declaring from his police court bench, heroically, that "nudity is no longer considered indecent."[15] (On the same night another magistrate had no difficulty charging nude dancers busted at Minsky's burlesque.)[16] And when the *Bremen* rioters came before him in early September, Brodsky seized on the opportunity to proclaim the values of America and denounce the Nazis. The swastika, he wrote, was a "black flag of piracy," and it stood for everything the United States opposed. To fly it was "a gratuitously brazen flaunting of an emblem which symbolizes all that is antithetical to American ideals of the God given and inalienable rights of all peoples to life, liberty and the pursuit of happiness.... [Nazism represents] a revolt against civilization—in brief, if I may borrow a biological concept, an atavistic throwback to pre-medieval, if not barbaric, social and political conditions."[17] These were stirring words, true in every particular; God bless Louis

Figure 1. From the Bradford Era newspaper, photo of Louis B. Brodsky, 1935.

Brodsky for uttering them; but it is far from clear that a police court magistrate had any business issuing any such opinion, or for that matter any clear basis in law for releasing the rioters.

In any case, Brodsky was Jewish, and his opinion was bait to the Nazis. The Roosevelt administration scrambled, once again, to disavow his action. The administration pressured New York Governor Herbert Lehman to declare that Brodsky had exceeded his authority, and Secretary of State Cordell Hull issued a formal apology to the Reich on the very day that the Nuremberg Laws were proclaimed.[18] But Minister of Propaganda Joseph Goebbels had already decided to use the Brodsky opinion for Nazi political purposes.

In fact, Brodsky's opinion was something of a propaganda gift to the Nazis: it provided them with a welcome opportunity to solidify their mastery over the Reich. Brodsky's opinion thrust him into the middle of a conflict over political symbolism in Nazi Germany. In September 1935, as the Nuremberg "Rally of Freedom" approached, the Nazi takeover of Germany was not yet symbolically complete. During the early period after Hitler's ascent to power in January 1933, the Nazi Party was forced to share authority with other right-wingers: nationalist conservatives, whose number included powerful figures such as President Paul von Hindenburg and former Chancellor Kurt von Schleicher. These were men who detested the democratic ways of the Weimar Republic, and who were willing to cooperate with the Nazis, but who maintained a degree of distance from the Nazi program. It was these nationalist conservatives who made the tragic miscalculation of placing Hitler in the Chancellorship of the Reich, confident that they could control him. As we all know, events rapidly proved them wrong: within weeks after Hitler took office on January 30, 1933, the Nazis were well on their way to full domination, in the course of the familiar nightmare sequence that marked Germany's descent into dictatorship: the Reichstag Fire of February 27, the elections of March 5, and finally the Enabling Act of March 24, which conferred dictatorial authority on Hitler.[19]

Nevertheless, both during and after these frightening developments, Hindenburg remained President, and even after his death in the summer of 1934, nationalist conservatives retained a role in the government of the Reich. Indeed, they enjoyed an official symbolic recognition of their right to a share of power in Germany: by a special decree of President Hindenburg, issued on March 12, 1933, whereas all other nations flew only one flag, the German Reich flew two flags together—on the one hand the swastika, described in Hindenburg's decree as representing "the mighty renaissance of the German nation" achieved by Nazism, and alongside it a plain flag with black, white, and red bars, described as representing "the glorious past of the German Reich," the symbolic territory of the more traditionalist right wing.[20] Carl Schmitt praised this peculiar two-faced national symbolism a means of "ceremoniously denying the Weimar system" without definitively raising one group of Weimar opponents over another. It conspicuously represented the limits of Nazi authority; as a matter of national symbolism, Germany was not yet *Nazi* Germany as long as both flags flew together; but it had the advantage of allowing the Nazis to claim the allegiance of the large numbers of German conservatives, particularly in the powerful bureaucracy, without insisting that they sign on fully to the radical Nazi program.[21]

By September 1935 the Nazis had made great progress in ridding themselves of the nationalist conservatives—sometimes indeed by murdering them, as they did Schleicher—but they were still compelled to share the symbolic stage, with both flags hoisted irksomely together. Brodsky's decision to release the rioters gave Goebbels his opening for eliminating the nationalist conservative symbol: "The Judge Broudski in New York," he wrote in his diary, "has insulted the German national flag.... Our answer: In Nuremberg the Reichstag will meet and declare the swastika flag to be our sole national flag."[22] Nuremberg would symbolically mark the definitive ascent of the Nazi Party to sole rule, and it would of course also be the occasion for turning the screws on Brodsky's fellow Jews in Germany: the "Party Rally of Freedom" would also serve as the occasion for the promulgation of two anti-Jewish laws, which had already been in active preparation for more than two years.

So it was that the Nuremberg Laws were offered to the world as a "reply" to an "insult" delivered by a Jewish magistrate in a Manhattan police court. But it is important to emphasize that they were not offered as a rejection of everything America stood for. It was perfectly possible to denounce the New York Jew Louis Brodsky without denouncing America. New York City, after all, as one German author observed in a 1935 book written in praise of FDR, had very little to do with "America": New York was a place where "the representatives of the races" gathered together to create a "mishmash of ideas and people," a place marked by a "great influence of the Jews," which made institutions like Columbia University centers of "radicalism." The true America, by contrast, was Anglo-Saxon and Protestant.[23] German racists had been saying similar derisive things about "Jewish" New York City for years.[24]

And indeed, once the rally convened, the Nazi leadership was careful to declare that its quarrel was with the Jews, not with the United States. Hitler made a point of pausing, in his address on the new laws, to praise the Roosevelt administration for its "thoroughly decent and honorable" disavowal of Brodsky;[25] the Nuremberg Laws, he explained, were intended simply to serve as a rebuke to "Jewish elements" everywhere, and as a confirmation of the "correctness" of National Socialism.[26] Göring, in his own speech formally presenting the new laws, added that Germany could only express its sympathy for the American people. After all, Americans, since they did not benefit from anti-Jewish laws of their own, had been "forced to witness" the indecent display of insolence by the "uppity Jew" Brodsky.[27]

Of course no Nazi speech should ever be taken at face value. Nevertheless the Nuremberg addresses of Hitler and Göring, with their studious effort to show respect toward the Roosevelt administration and their nasty bid for the support of American anti-Semites, fit with what we know from many other sources: in 1935 Nazi attitudes toward the United States had by no means yet hardened into unambiguous hostility, any more than Washington was yet ready to write off coexistence with Hitler. In the careful judgment of historian Philipp Gassert, for example, it was only

Figure 2. The gathering of the Reichstag for the promulgation of the Nuremberg Laws. *Source:* Ullstein Bild © Getty Images.

beginning in 1936 at the very earliest, and especially in 1937, that the United States would "finally los[e] its role as a model" in Nazi Germany.[28]

That is not to suggest that relations between the two countries were wholly harmonious in the early 1930s, or that the Nazis saw nothing to hate. It is certainly true that the American press ran many ugly stories about what was going on in Germany, and those stories certainly distressed the Nazi leadership. It is true that the Nazis abhorred the "American ideals of the God given and inalienable rights of all peoples to life, liberty and the pursuit of happiness" of which Brodsky spoke. Nevertheless, in the first years of Nazi rule there remained a widespread sense in Germany that the United

States was at heart a kindred "Nordic" polity, even if it was one that remained attached to obsolete liberal and democratic forms, and one that might yet succumb to the dangers of race mixing.

As a result it can be, in fact, a thoroughly jarring experience to read German accounts of America from these years. Consider, for example, Albrecht Wirth. Wirth, in his 1934 *Völkisch World History*, a global history for Nazi readers, with a stock portrait of Hitler as its frontispiece, described America for his German readers in these terms in his opening pages: "The most important event in the history of the states of the Second Millennium—up until the [First World] War—was the founding of the United States of America. The struggle of the Aryans for world domination received thereby its strongest prop."[29] Modern Americans sometimes have ugly things to say about the Founding; we all understand, as Thurgood Marshall ruefully said, that the American Constitution "was defective from the start, requiring several amendments, a civil war, and momentous social transformation to attain . . . its respect for the individual freedoms and human rights, that we hold as fundamental today";[30] we all know that many of the Founders held beliefs that we now find reprehensible, but it still takes one's breath away a bit to find a Nazi describing the Founding as a historic turning point in "the Aryan struggle for world domination."

Nor was Wirth alone; he was reciting a standard tenet of Nazi world history in the early 1930s. According to Wahrhold Drascher, for example, author of a handsomely printed 1936 tome titled *The Supremacy of the White Race*, the Founding was "the first fateful turning point" in the worldwide rise of white supremacy;[31] America had assumed "the leadership of the white peoples" after World War I, fulfilling the promise of centuries of American racism,[32] and if it were not for the contribution of the Americans "a conscious unity of the white race would never have emerged."[33] Such sentiments were echoed, for example, by the leading Nazi

ideologue Alfred Rosenberg in 1933.[34] Or as Hitler himself put
it, in a ringing passage, "The racially pure and still unmixed German has risen to become master of the American continent, and he
will remain the master, as long as he does not fall victim to racial
pollution."[35]

To be sure, we must keep our composure when we encounter
Nazi pronouncements about America like these (and the many
more from which I will quote in the following pages). If there was
a great deal of praise for American white supremacy in Germany in
the early 1930s, it was also commonplace to speculate the United
States might well fail to achieve its historic racist mission. Even the
Nazis most favorably inclined were unsure that they could count
on American friendship in the long term.[36] When the *National Socialist Monthly* published a special number on "The U.S.A. and Us"
in November 1933, for example, it trumpeted Germany's affinities
with the Americans at some points; but at others it voiced uncertainty about the future course of American development, as well
as expressing anger at the ugly stories the American press had published.[37] If the Nazis often voiced their sense of kinship with the
United States, they were nevertheless never quite sure what they
were dealing with.

Still, it remains the case that Nazi authors of the period were
quite conscious of the racist strain in American law and society, and
sometimes loud in their praise; and it was commonplace throughout the era of the making of the Nuremberg Laws to treat the
United States not as an inevitable ideological blood enemy, but as
a forerunner and even a potential fellow traveler. When Nazi observers looked out on early New Deal America, they saw a country
where white supremacy ran deep, at least once the visitor left New
York City behind. And while it is hard to know how many "Anglo-
Saxon" Americans would have been receptive to Göring's speech in
1935, there were certainly many who did indeed regard people like
Brodsky as "uppity Jews."

As for the two new Nazi anti-Jewish measures that we remember today as the Nuremberg Laws, they were crafted in an atmosphere marked by the same tentative and uncertain spirit of kinship with America: hard though it may be for us to accept it today, the Nuremberg Laws were the product of many months of Nazi discussion and debate that included regular, studious, and often admiring engagement with the race law of the United States.

THE SECOND NUREMBERG LAW: MAKING NAZI CITIZENS

The two anti-Jewish measures we call the Nuremberg Laws today, and whose text was read out by Hermann Göring at the Party Rally of Freedom, are so brief that their principal provisions can be quoted in full. As the *New York Times* correctly reported, the first of them, the *Reichsbürgergesetz*, the Reich Citizenship Law, commonly called the Citizenship Law, established a distinction between "citizens of the Reich" (*Reichsbürger*) and mere "nationals" (*Staatsangehörige*). Its aim was to restrict full political rights to members of the German *Volk*, the mystically understood national German race community (adjective form *völkisch*):

Reich Citizenship Law

§ 1

(1) A national [*Staatsangehöriger*] is any person who belongs to the mutual protection association [*Schutzverband*] of the German Reich, and who owes special duties in return.

(2) Nationality [*Staatsangehörigkeit*] is acquired through the provisions of the Law on Membership in the Reich and the State.

§ 2

(1) A Reich citizen is exclusively a national of German blood, or racially related blood, who demonstrates through his conduct that he is willing and suited to faithfully serve the German *Volk* and Reich.

(2) The right of Reich citizenship is acquired through the conferral of the brevet of Reich citizenship.

(3) The Reich citizen is the sole bearer of full political rights, to be exercised according to the measure of the laws.[38]

The second, the *Gesetz zum Schutze des deutschen Blutes und der deutschen Ehre*, the Law on the Protection of German Blood and German Honor, commonly called the Blood Law, banned mixed marriages and sexual relations between Jews and Germans, as well as the employment by Jews of German women as household servants. It made two distinct provisions about mixed marriages: first, that they were void as a matter of civil law, and, second, that they constituted a criminal offense. (The Blood Law also included a sarcastic provision permitting Jews to fly their own Jewish flag; when Göring read that provision out at the rally, the assembled Reichstag delegates, it is reported, "roared with laughter.")[39] The Blood Law left unresolved the difficult question of who counted as a "Jew."

Law on the Protection of German Blood and German Honor

Deeply moved by the recognition that purity of German blood is the prerequisite for the continued existence of the German *Volk*, and inspired by the unbending will to secure the German nation for all time to come, the Reichstag has unanimously voted the following law, which is hereby promulgated:

§ 1

(1) Marriages between Jews and nationals of German blood or racially related blood are forbidden. If such marriages are nevertheless entered into they are null and void, even if they are concluded abroad in order to evade this law.

(2) Actions to nullify such marriages are brought by the state prosecutor.

§ 2

Extramarital intercourse between Jews and nationals of German blood or racially related blood is forbidden.

§ 3

Jews may not employ female nationals of German blood or racially related blood under the age of 45 years in their household.

§ 4

(1) Jews are forbidden to raise the Reich and National flag, and to display the colors of the Reich.

(2) However they are permitted to display Jewish colors. The exercise of this right stands under the protection of the state.

§ 5

(1) Any person who violates the prohibition of § 1 shall be punished by imprisonment at hard labor.[40]

(2) Any male person who violates the prohibition of § 2 shall be punished either by ordinary imprisonment or by imprisonment at hard labor.

(3) Any person who violates the prohibitions of §§ 3 or 4 shall be punished by ordinary imprisonment for up to a year and by a fine, or by either of these penalties.[41]

After Göring had finished reading these ugly decrees, reported the *New York Herald Tribune*, a Republican newspaper that was one of the few in America to headline the racism of the Nuremberg Laws, the assembled Reichstag members, "six-hundred odd men, the bulk of them in brown uniforms, leapt to their feet" in a display of enthusiasm.[42]

The question we must ask is whether the Nazis gleaned any American inspiration in the making of this program of persecution. Here it is essential that we begin by posing the question correctly. We must recognize what the Nuremberg Laws did not say, and conversely what American law of the era did say. The Nuremberg Laws did not aim to set up a system of segregation or apartheid. Their twofold purpose was to create a new Nazi law of citizenship, alongside a new Nazi law of sex and intermarriage, which I will call by the American name "miscegenation." As for America, citizenship and miscegenation were both central to American interwar race law. Segregation was only a part of it.[43]

The last point deserves some emphasis. When Americans think about their legal history of race today, they can find it hard to shake off the fascination with Jim Crow segregation in the South. In the 1950s *Brown v. Board of Education* became the pivot on which our understanding of modern American race law turned;[44] and we have commonly framed American race questions around the conflict between *Brown* and *Plessy v. Ferguson* ever since.[45] In the American collective memory, race law involves first and foremost separate schools, separate water fountains, seating at the back of the bus, and so on—the practices that triggered the great sit-ins, protests, and violent clashes of the early civil rights era. The identification of race law with segregation has shaped all of the English-language literature on American influence in Germany; that is why, when scholars have wondered whether American race law influenced the Nazis, what they have wondered about is the significance of "American segregation laws."[46] But there was always much more to American race law than segregation, as Europeans of the interwar period well knew; and we will not understand how Nazi lawyers viewed "Nordic" America unless we bear that fact in mind.

American race law, pre-*Brown*, sprawled over a wide range of technically distinct legal areas, including not only "separate but equal" segregation under the rule of *Plessy*, but also Indian law,[47] anti-Chinese and -Japanese legislation,[48] and disabilities in civil procedure and election law.[49] America was particularly notable for its creation of novel forms of de facto and de jure second-class citizenship for blacks, Native Americans, Filipinos, and Puerto Ricans.[50] Anti-miscegenation laws on the state level featured especially prominently;[51] they would be eliminated only at the tail end of the civil rights era, with *Loving v. Virginia* in 1967.[52] So did immigration and naturalization law on the federal level;[53] de facto race-based immigration and naturalization practices would survive until the Immigration and Nationality Act of 1965, which came into full effect only in 1968.[54] Some aspects of this extensive body of American race law were closely linked to eugenics; immigration and anti-miscegenation laws in particular were often described as measures related to the eugenic maintenance of a racially healthy population.[55] Other aspects, however, like segregation and the creation of forms of second-class citizenship, had nothing to do with eugenics as such. They represented a different mode of exclusion and persecution, involving legal degradation rather than population engineering.

And in all of these areas the United States stood out for the energy and innovativeness of its law. Early twentieth-century America was the global leader in race law, admired around the world for the vigor of its legislation; in this the Nazis were not alone. As in so many areas, this was one where American creativity shone.

AMERICA: THE GLOBAL LEADER IN RACIST IMMIGRATION LAW

American anti-miscegenation law is a topic for the next chapter. For now, I begin with the American law of immigration, naturalization, and citizenship.

To some extent, what Nazi lawyers found intriguing about America extended back to the same Founding Era that was highlighted by Nazi world historians. America, as Nazi authors knew, had a history of racial exclusionism that dated to the earliest years of the Republic: When the first Congress met, among its many historic enactments was the Naturalization Act of 1790, which opened naturalization to "any alien, being a free white person."[56] This was, as a Nazi commentator observed in 1936, an unusual measure for the time: racial restrictions were not unheard of in the eighteenth century, but they were not common.[57]

For the most part, though, the America that appealed to the Nazis (and other European racists as well) was the America of the late nineteenth and early twentieth centuries. As one leading Nazi author summarized American immigration history in 1933, "[u]ntil the 1880s, a liberal freedom-oriented conception led the United States to regard itself as the refuge of all oppressed peoples, and consequently limitations on immigration, to say nothing of bans on immigration, were considered irreconcilable with the 'free' Constitution."[58] That is not to say that there were no restrictions at all before the 1880s. In the antebellum period a number of states, especially in the Midwest, introduced legislation aiming to prevent free blacks from settling,[59] while in the 1850s Connecticut and Massachusetts introduced literacy tests in the hope of keeping undesirable Irish immigrants at bay without formally excluding them.[60] Nevertheless, taken in the large, the United States was a country of open borders during the first two-thirds of the nineteenth century, and of course it was a country that attracted large migrations from Europe.

Beginning in the late 1870s, however, American immigration and naturalization law took a different turn. The shift had to do largely with the appearance of Asian immigrants.[61] Late nineteenth-century American immigration legislation was directed in particular against Asians,[62] beginning especially with the Chinese exclusion legislation in California in the 1870s,[63] and on the national level in 1882.[64] Would-be Japanese immigrants were targeted as well, in a history of many decades that gave rise to dangerous diplomatic friction between the Japanese Empire and the United States.[65] But by the end of the century, exclusionist campaigns began slowly to move beyond the perceived problems of Asian immigration to focus on Europe as well. An especially important 1896 bill aimed to restrict immigration through the use of literacy tests.[66] That legislation was vetoed by President Cleveland,[67] but it was followed by a series of twentieth-century measures. First came the Asiatic Barred Zone Act of 1917, which (as it name suggests) marked out a vast area of Asia as the home of undesirables, to be barred alongside homosexuals, idiots, anarchists, and more.[68] That was followed by two major pieces of "national origins" immigration and naturalization law: the Emergency Quota Act of 1921[69] and the Immigration Act of 1924.[70] The latter in particular was manifestly "race-based," favoring "the 'Nordics' of northern and western

Europe over the 'undesirable races' of eastern and southern Europe."[71]

It is important to note that the United States was not alone in introducing such measures. In particular, as the Nazis were very much aware, America was part of a broader historically British world. British imperialism deposited a network of "free white men's democracies" around the globe, displaying a common commitment to maintaining what Columbia professor J. W. Burgess influentially praised in 1890 as "ethnically homogeneous" states.[72] These included Canada and New Zealand;[73] Australia, home of anti-Chinese agitation linked to similar agitation in California beginning in the late 1840s;[74] and of course South Africa.[75] A British demographer described this Anglophone world in 1936 this way: "[T]here are few gaps in the ring fence which has been erected in the last 50 years by the United States and the Dominions in order to exclude non-Europeans."[76] As we shall see, the Nazis knew this Anglophone pattern well, and looked for their models not only in the United States, but more broadly in the British Dominions.

Nevertheless by the latter part of the nineteenth century, it was the United States that occupied the place at the vanguard, in the eyes of Germans and others as well. From the late nineteenth century onward the United States came to be regarded as "the leader in developing explicitly racist policies of nationality and immigration,"[77] and American immigration and naturalization practices were attracting plenty of notice in Europe well before the emergence of the Nazi movement.

Some of the attention came from Europeans on the left who deplored the American developments. Hostile commentary was particularly noticeable in the French literature: French observers, with their own republican tradition of "liberty, equality, and fraternity," were often taken aback by the frank racism of American democracy. When the French social thinker André Siegfried published his study of American society in 1927, for example, he treated immigration policy as fundamental to the workings of a disturbing broader pattern of American racism.[78] Other French authors saw America similarly.[79]

But there were also foreigners who looked more favorably on the American experiments. American immigration law was influential throughout the Anglophone world,[80] and it attracted continental Europeans as well.[81] It is particularly important that American immigration law caught the attention of one influential book: the late nineteenth-century *Handbook of the Jewish Question* by Theodor Fritsch. Fritsch was the man responsible for publishing the German editions of both *The Protocols of the Elders of Zion* and the anti-Semitic writings of Henry Ford. This figure, one of the guiding lights of German anti-Semitism, featured the United States in the opening pages of his *Handbook*, which would be reprinted over and over again in the Nazi period. Late nineteenth-century America was a country, wrote Fritsch, that had finally learned the error of its egalitarian ways: "America, soaked in ideas of freedom and equality, has hitherto accorded equal rights to all races. But it finds itself compelled to revise its attitudes and its laws and create restrictions on Negroes and Chinese."[82] To Fritsch, the history of American immigration law offered a parable on the dangers of ignoring race in favor of a foolish egalitarianism. As we shall see shortly, Hitler and other Nazis would often repeat Fritsch's interpretive line.

AMERICAN SECOND-CLASS CITIZENSHIP

Immigration and naturalization law was only part of what made the United States a late nineteenth-century leader. Alongside it came American citizenship law. Over the same decades of the late nineteenth century, the United States was developing some distinctive forms of second-class citizenship. Mark Mazower summarizes some of these forms, and speculates that the American law of second-class citizenship would have been of interest to Nazi lawyers as they set out to create their own form of second-class citizenship for Jews at Nuremberg: "Inside the USA (whose racial laws and eugenics movement had earned Hitler's praise in the 1920s) native Americans were viewed up to 1924 as 'nationals' but not citizens—a distinction that late nineteenth-century American commentators acknowledged to be the prerogative of 'a great colonial power'; Puerto Ricans were defined constitutionally much as the Germans later did the Czechs— they were 'foreign to the United States in a domestic sense.'"[83] Mazower is right: he is right, as we shall see shortly, that Hitler, following in the footsteps of Theodor Fritsch, admired American race law; and he is right that the treatment of Native Americans and Puerto Ricans, both carefully discussed in the German legal literature,[84] offered models of second-class citizenship that intrigued Nazi policy makers. But the full story also includes two other especially important populations, Filipinos and especially American blacks.

Especially American blacks. The problem of black citizenship is a very old one in America, with a history too long and complex to be rehearsed here. What matters most for my purposes, and what mattered most to Nazi observers, were the developments in the creation of second-class forms of black citizenship that dated, once again, to the later decades of the nineteenth century. During the antebellum period, blacks were denied citizenship status in one of the most reviled decisions in American constitutional history, *Dred Scott v. Sandford*,[85] which was instrumental in triggering the Civil War.[86] After the victory of the North, *Dred Scott* was overturned, as black citizenship status was in principle guaranteed by the Fourteenth and Fifteenth Amendments.[87] But with the collapse of Reconstruction, blacks, especially but not exclusively southern ones, were deprived of meaningful political rights by a host of late nineteenth-century legal subterfuges, designed to evade the strictures of the post–Civil War Constitution.

The right to vote in particular was denied to virtually all southern blacks. The techniques involved included, notably, literacy tests, a device that had first been used by Connecticut and Massachusetts in the 1850s as a means of introducing covert racial restrictions in immigration.[88] Literacy tests were a clever and influential American legal invention, imitated by the Australians in their own racially restrictive immigration legislation of 1901, and recommended by the influential James Bryce for the Anglophone world more broadly.[89] Alongside literacy tests came "grandfather clauses,"[90] limiting voting rights to those whose ancestors had voted before emancipation, poll taxes, and more, including the creation of a system of political primaries that guaranteed exclusive rule to the Southern Democratic Party.[91] The Supreme Court did not hesitate to validate such stratagems, despite the guarantees of the Reconstruction Amendments.[92] The net result was that American blacks, while de jure citizens, were de facto second class.

Here again Europeans, and Germans in particular, took note. In fact, the black second-class citizenship in America was a source of real fascination for leading German intellectuals in the decades before the Nazis' rise to power. Max Weber was one of them. "Within American democracy," wrote Weber in a 1906 newspaper essay, using an excitable exclamation point, equal voting rights were rights for "non-coloreds! since for Negroes and all racial mongrels [*Mischlinge*] they *de facto* do not exist."[93] (Weber believed this was a typical product of the Protestant ethic in America.)[94] Weber was by no means the only major figure to take an interest in this aspect of American racism. Eduard Meyer, the immensely erudite ancient historian, published a book about America that explained the relevant practices in careful detail: "All means are used to render the Negro's right to vote illusory," he wrote, surveying the wealth of legal devices invented by Americans.[95] "The English-speaking Americans," observed the eminent sociologist Robert Michels, "deny the Negro any form of equal rights";[96] he too worked through the legal details. Early twentieth-century German authors regularly observed that the political rights of American blacks were, as standard texts reported, a "dead letter";[97] despite the guarantees of the Reconstruction Amendments, those political rights had been "withdrawn";[98] without ever saying so openly, the southern states had made black voting rights a nullity.[99]

De facto black disenfranchisement may have been the most striking and noticeable aspect of race-based second-class citizenship law in turn-of-the-century America, but it was not the only one. Also of considerable importance in the making of American second-class citizenship was the now widely forgotten case of the Puerto Ricans and Filipinos. Victory in the Spanish-American War in 1898 brought the United States colonial possessions in Puerto Rico and the Philippines. The consequence was a minor crisis in American constitutional law. America had never sought the sort of overseas imperial power that the European countries had been accumulating, and the Fourteenth Amendment seemed to leave little room for the creation of a class of colonial subjects. When America acquired new territories, the inhabitants were supposed to become citizens. Nevertheless there was widespread sentiment against granting the inhabitants of the new territories full citizenship. The Philippines in particular, which became the site of a nasty American war, was home to a Pacific population that Americans regarded as belonging to an inferior, or at least for the moment hopelessly backward, race. In a series of decisions known as the Insular Cases, the Supreme Court consented to the creation of a de jure form of second-class citizenship for the newly conquered populations: the Constitution, held the Court, permitted these colonial subjects to be treated as mere "non-citizen nationals."[100]

The Insular Cases are little remembered by ordinary Americans today, but they were a subject of intense interest at the end of the nineteenth century and beginning of the twentieth, and contemporary legal scholars highlight them as a key development in American race law and the making of an "American Empire."[101] Europeans too paid attention: the struggles of democratic America with the creation of subject status for colonized peoples were a matter of international interest in the age of European imperialism.[102] In particular early twentieth-century Germans, including some very prominent scholars, created a substantial literature on American colonial law in the decades before the Nazis came to power.[103]

Perhaps the most striking of these German students of American second-class citizenship law was Erich Kaufmann, one of the most eminent, and controversial, German Jewish lawyers of the twentieth century. Kaufmann, a brilliant professor of public and international law, was a man who felt the pull of the German far right wing in the 1920s. He associated with proto-fascists in Weimar, and after the Nazis took power he hung on in Nazi Germany until 1938. Surviving the war in hiding, he returned after 1945 to take up a prominent professorship (despite the fact that the American authorities described him as "unsuited for the indoctrination of German youth with the values of democracy").[104] This figure from the eerie world of the interwar right wing, one of a number of leading Jewish intellectuals whose political sympathies could draw them "precariously close" to the orbit of fascism,[105] made the American colonial experience the subject of his first book in 1908.

Kaufmann's book described at great and admiring length how America, having been called to the historic task of a "colonial expansion of its possessions and its sovereignty,"[106] had confronted the question of "whether an uncivilized population ... can be governed according to the norms guaranteed by the Constitution to superior [hochstehenden] citizens."[107] Kaufmann devoted attentive energy to describing the work of the Supreme Court in the Insular Cases, and registered his deep respect for the subtlety of American judges and the "wealth of life and immediacy" to be found in the American common law. The early twentieth century witnessed the rise of a cult of a kind of common-law worship in Germany,[108] and Kaufmann clearly participated in it:

> At first glance, the picture that [the Insular Cases] offers to us is exceedingly motley, and almost confusing, especially to an eye that is accustomed to German decisional law. As we study it more deeply and reflect on it in an unbiased way, however, we must concede that there is a wealth of life and immediacy in these decisions, a thorough intellectual and juristic examination of the material from the most varied points of view, a penetrating recourse to the ultimate questions, an impartial formulation of the arguments for and against, and a proud appeal to the living legal intuitions of the American people that lie behind them, which reveals the high legal and political talents and the cultivation of the people of the Union.[109]

As we shall see, Nazi jurists too would see much to admire in the "life and immediacy" of American common-law racism and the "living legal intuitions" of the American people on which it was founded.

Kaufmann was not the only prominent commentator on the American colonial experience and its legal consequences. Two famous scholars, the German Hugo Münsterberg at Harvard and the Germanophile Ernst Freund at the University of Chicago, published books in German recounting the American adventures in colonial conquest and law.[110] Freund in particular explained how the United States had created a new category of "subjects without citizenship rights";[111] in so doing, he explained, America had invented a novel form of law closely analogous to early nineteenth-century state statutes barring free blacks and the late nineteenth-century statutes barring the Chinese. America was pioneering a range of forms of race-based second-class citizenship.[112] There was other commentary as well: as a leading German journal reported a couple of years before World War I, in language that anticipated the Nuremberg Laws, Puerto Ricans and Filipinos had been subjected to the status of "Schutzbürger zweiter Klasse," second-class citizens entitled to the protection of the state, but not to full political rights.[113] America, in the eyes of this German literature, was a laboratory for experimentation in diminished citizenship rights.

THE NAZIS PICK UP THE THREAD

Thus the Nazi movement emerged in a Europe familiar with American immigration and second-class citizenship law, and sometimes fascinated by it; and the familiarity and sometime fascination accompanied the early development of Nazism as well, and continued into the years of the making of the Citizenship Law proclaimed at Nuremberg.

In tracking the Nazi strain in the European engagement with American race law, the place to begin is with the movement's bible, Hitler's *Mein Kampf*. The second volume of *Mein Kampf*, published in 1927, laid out Hitler's vision for German renewal. That vision drew broadly on the Nazi Party Program of 1920, five of whose twenty-five points involved citizenship. The 1920 Party Program called for sharp limits on citizenship, which was to be restricted to persons of "German blood," along with a scheme of disabilities for resident foreigners, who were to be threatened with expulsion:

4. Only a *Volk*-comrade [*Volksgenosse*] can be a citizen [*Staatsbürger*]. Only a person of German blood, without regard to religion, can be a *Volk*-comrade. Accordingly no Jew can be a *Volk*-comrade.

5. Any person who is not a citizen should be able to live in Germany merely as a guest, and must be subject to legislation for foreigners.

6. Only a citizen is permitted the right to decide on the leadership [*Führung*] and laws of the state. Therefore we demand that every public office, regardless of what kind, regardless of whether it is an office of the Reich, of the constituent States of the Reich, or any municipality, be accessible only to citizens. . . .

7. We demand that the state obligate itself to provide the opportunities and wherewithal of life in the first instance strictly for citizens. If it is not possible to provide sustenance for the entire population, then nationals of foreign countries (non-citizens) must be expelled from the Reich.

8. All further immigration of non-Germans is to be prevented. We demand that all non-Germans who have immigrated into Germany since August 2, 1914, be immediately compelled to leave the Reich.[114]

These demands, which anticipate so much of the far-right agitation that is troubling Europe again today, established the propositions that would be fundamental to Nazi citizenship law as it emerged at Nuremberg in 1935.

In Volume 2 of *Mein Kampf* Hitler built on the 1920 Party Program, developing a more elaborate conception of race-based citizenship. But as he turned to the citizenship problem in 1927, Hitler was able to seize on a source of authority that had not been available in 1920, in the form of the new American immigration statutes of 1921 and 1924. The Nazi leader certainly saw things to dislike about the United States in this period, hating Woodrow Wilson, the architect of the Peace of Versailles, and detecting the lurking influence of Jews in much of American society.[115] But it is a striking fact that praise for American race policies, and envy of American power, predominated in his pronouncements in the late 1920s, particularly when it came to American immigration legislation. Hitler too, like so many Europeans before him, regarded the United States as the obvious "leader in developing explicitly racist policies of nationality and immigration." His treatment of citizenship in *Mein Kampf* began with a characteristically sarcastic account of the state of German law:

> Today the right of citizenship is acquired primarily through birth *inside* the borders of the state. Race or membership in the *Volk* play no role whatsoever. A Negro who previously lived in the German protectorates and now resides in Germany can thus beget a "German citizen." By the same token any Jewish child, or Polish child, or African child, or Asian child can become a German citizen without further ado.

> Apart from naturalization through birth there is also the possibility of subsequent naturalization.... Racial considerations play no role in this whatsoever.

> The entire process of the acquisition of citizenship is hardly different from joining an automobile club.

After demanding the acquisition of citizenship take a more meaningful and elevated race-based form, Hitler then turned to the only example on the international scene of a praiseworthy order:

> There is currently one state in which one can observe at least weak beginnings of a better conception. This is of course not

our exemplary German Republic, but the American Union, in which an effort is being made to consider the dictates of reason to at least some extent. The American Union categorically refuses the immigration of physically unhealthy elements, and simply excludes the immigration of certain races. In these respects America already pays obeisance, at least in tentative first steps, to the characteristic *völkisch* conception of the state.[116]

American legal scholars have written a great deal about the racism of the 1920s immigration statutes; but they seem not to have taken notice of the startling fact that those statutes were lauded by Hitler himself as the prime, and indeed only, example of *völkisch* citizenship legislation in the 1920s.[117]

Hitler continued to speak in such terms thereafter, repeating his judgment of American immigration law in 1928: Americans felt the need, he wrote, deploying standard Nazi terminology, to exclude the "foreign body" of "strangers to the blood" of the ruling race; that was the felt need that was expressed in their immigration legislation.[118] He made similar declarations in his "Second Book," the unpublished sequel to *Mein Kampf* that he drafted in 1928.[119] The "Second Book" is indeed striking for its depiction of America as a racial model for, and future racial rival of, Europe. Some German racists in the 1920s portrayed the United States as a country gravely endangered by race mixing, all too likely to go into decline unless "the good blood in the Union" could hold off the onslaught of "a chaos of *Völker* made up of Negroes, Jews, southern Europeans, mongrels, yellows, and undefinables from the milk-coffee Lands."[120] Not so Hitler. By contrast with these fellow racists, the Hitler of the "Second Book" was notably sanguine about American prospects.[121] Developments in American immigration law, he held, demonstrated that Americans had seen the light:

The capacity of assimilation for the American Union has given out, both with regard to the Chinese as well as with regard to the Japanese element. People feel this clearly and know it and for that reason they would most prefer to exclude these foreign bodies from immigration. In this way American immigration policies provide confirmation that the previous "melting pot" approach presupposes humans of a certain similar racial basis and immediately fails as soon as fundamentally different types of humans are involved. That the American Union feels itself to be a Nordic-German state and by no means an international *Völker*-porridge is also revealed by the apportionment of immigration quotas among the European *Völker*. Scandinavians, that is to say, Swedes, Norwegians, furthermore Danes, then Englishmen and finally Germans have been accorded the largest contingent. Latins and slavs receive very little, and the Japanese and Chinese are groups that one would prefer to exclude entirely.[122]

The happy result of the shift in immigration policies, Hitler concluded, was that America had safeguarded its character as a "Nordic" state; Europe, he warned, could not hope to compete unless it did the same.[123] This was the same year in which Hitler was proclaiming his admiration for the American conquest of the West, where the Americans had "gunned down the millions of Redskins to a few hundred thousand";[124] this too, he said, offered yet another "Nordic" example that the Europeans would do well to follow. Assessing some of these writings of the 1920s, historian Detlef Junker concludes that for Hitler, America was "*the* model of a state organized on principles of *Rasse* and *Raum*," on principles of race and the acquisition of territory for a racially defined *Volk*.[125] Gassert too holds that Hitler regarded the America of the 1920s, with its unapologetically race-based immigration legislation and its epic "Aryan" colonization of the West, as a "race state" that deserved admiration.[126]

The views of the Führer on the subject of the "race state," it goes without saying, carried immense weight in Nazi Germany.[127] Hitler's discussion of American immigration law in *Mein Kampf* in particular would be cited whenever Nazi jurists discussed problems of citizenship after the Nazis took the reins in 1933,[128] and it set the tone that remained dominant in Nazi writings on American law throughout the early thirties:[129] America was a country that was in some ways weak, and its future as a racist order was perhaps uncertain, but it remained the leading example of a jurisdiction groping its way toward a race law of the kind essential to the creation of a *völkisch* state, most especially through its sage immigration restrictions. As the *National Socialist Monthly* put it in November 1933, echoing *Mein Kampf* and Fritsch's *Handbook of the Jewish Question*, "The United States of the new world have come to understand the monstrous danger of the 'great melting pot of races' over the course of the last decades, and put a check on bastardization through draconian immigration law. . . . To these circles of tribally related Americans we reach out our hand in friendship."[130] America, as Hitler had written, had taken the tentative first steps; the moment had come for the torch to pass to Nazi Germany, and the hope of a spiritual alliance between Nazi Germany and the white supremacist United States was not to be excluded.

TOWARD THE CITIZENSHIP LAW:
NAZI POLITICS IN THE EARLY 1930S

Before turning to the nuts and bolts of Nazi-era investigation of America's immigration and citizenship law, it is important to set the stage by establishing some context about the goals of the Nazi regime after it took power. In particular it is essential to emphasize that extermination of the Jews was not the initial aim of the Nazis. In the early years of the Nazi regime "deportation and annihilation" were as yet "difficult to imagine";[131] the aim that always stood "in the foreground" was to drive Jews to emigrate, whether through violence on the street or through the creation of legal disabilities.[132] The goals of the early 1930s were nicely formulated by Wilhelm Stuckart, coauthor of the standard commentary on the Nuremberg Laws. Stuckart, later a high SS officer, would be present at the Wannsee Conference that decided on the Final Solution, and was eventually tried as a war criminal.[133] But in the early 1930s he spoke not of the "*Final* Solution" (*Endlösung*), but of the "*definitive* solution to the Jewish problem" (*endgültige Lösung*):

> The two Nuremberg Laws [i.e., the Citizenship Law and the Blood Law] represent the beginning of the definitive solution to the Jewish Problem in Germany. Starting from the recognition that Jewdom involves, not a religious community, but a community of persons related by blood—a community that is worlds apart from the German *Volk*—these laws, and the supplementary ordinances and provisions for their execution, complete the legal separation of Germandom and Jewdom in the most important realms of life. It has been made forever impossible for Jewdom to mix itself [*Vermischung*] with the German *Volk*, or to get mixed up [*Einmischung*] in state policy, economic policy or cultural shaping of Germany. If according to the principles laid down in these Laws the Jews still belong to the mutual protection association of the Reich and remain nationals for the time being, the definitive solution to the Jewish question can nevertheless only consist in the territorial separation of the Jews from the German *Volk*: i.e. the goal of German Jewish policy is the emigration of the Jews out of Germany.[134]

Annihilation came later; in the period of concern for this book, the Nazi policy was coerced emigration.

We must bear that fact in mind as we try to understand Nazi citizenship law and its relation to developments in the United States. For a regime whose aim was to drive those of supposedly "foreign blood" to emigrate, citizenship law was centrally important. Correspondingly, after taking power, the Nazis moved quickly to alter German citizenship law in order to disfavor Jews and other "foreign bodies." The project began on July 14, 1933, with a Law on the Revocation of Naturalization and the Withdrawal of German Citizenship, promulgated on the same day as the basic Nazi eugenics statute.[135] The main purpose of this first Nazi citizenship law was to facilitate the denaturalization and expulsion of *Ostjuden*, Eastern European Jews who had arrived after the First World War.[136] Reich Minister of the Interior Wilhelm Frick described it as "the beginning and point of departure for German race legislation";[137] and the next two years of debate and pressure consistently emphasized the fundamental role of citizenship law, culminating in the Nuremberg Citizenship Law that definitively assigned Jews to second-class status.

And it is an unpleasant truth that throughout this effort to degrade, demonize, and expel the Jews of Germany, American law remained a regular Nazi point of reference, just as it had been for Hitler before. America remained the leader, and the Nazis repeatedly turned to the American example when developing their own immigration and citizenship law.

After his ascent to the Chancellorship, Hitler himself ceased holding forth on technical legal questions. But leading Nazi jurists and functionaries picked up the thread, maintaining a steady and regularly reiterated interest in American examples. An important early example is Otto Koellreutter, perhaps the most eminent Nazi public lawyer in the early 1930s. A sympathizer of the Nazis from 1930 onward, Koellreutter formally joined the party on May 1, 1933, the same day that Carl Schmitt joined. In that same year he was given a Chair of Public Law in Munich, the home city of the Nazis. He served in leading academic positions, as journal editor and the like.[138]

In late 1933 this high priest of juristic Nazism published a book intended to lay out the basics of public law for what the Nazis were calling their "National Revolution." Public law included immigration and naturalization; and when Koellreutter came to that subject he devoted a long discussion to the American example. He began by touching on the British Dominions as well as the United States. As Nazi writers noted, the British imperial world had "unwritten social laws" against race mixing, which they certainly found of interest, and a few formal laws as well.[139] The Nazi interest in Anglophone traditions deserves to be flagged: The Nazis were drawing on practices that had developed in the broader historically British world, not just in the United States. Still, what intrigued Koellreutter most was the legislation of America. He wrote,

> *A further necessary measure for maintaining the healthy racial cohesion of the* Volk *lies in the regulation of immigration.* In this connection it is above all the legislation of the United States and of the British Dominions that has yielded interesting results.

Worthy of attention above all is the development of immigration legislation in the United States. Until the 1880s, a liberal freedom-oriented conception led the United States to regard itself as the refuge of all oppressed peoples, and consequently limitations on immigration, to say nothing of bans on immigration, were considered irreconcilable with the "free" Constitution. This conception very quickly changed. 1879 witnessed the first bills aimed at banning Chinese immigration. However it was above all after the World War that American immigration legislation embarked on an entirely new path. Today that legislation represents a carefully thought-through system that first of all protects the United States from the eugenic point of view against inferior elements trying to immigrate.... [Regulations targeting physically inferior and unhealthy would-be immigrants] are applied strictly, and even harshly.

Alongside eugenic measures is the establishment by law of certain immigration quotas. For the World War awakened American consciousness to the fact that it is by no means the case that all immigrants can be melded in equal measure into the originally Anglo-Saxon population, and that a fully free immigration policy must inevitably endanger the stamp of the national American type. So came into the being in 1921 the first Quota Law, in which each European country was credited with a certain number of immigrants, and indeed no more than 3% of the number of immigrants from the country in question who had settled in the United States in 1910. So for example in 1924 there were 165,000 immigrants, among them 62,000 English and Irish, 51,000 Germans, 3845 Italians and 2248 Russians including the East European Jews. In the last several years immigration has been even further limited.[140]

Two observations about this passage are warranted. First, it was carefully researched. As this and other passages soon to be quoted show, Germans were giving studious scholarly attention to American immigration law.

Second, it is impossible to characterize what Koellreutter wrote as intended for foreign consumption. Scholars who want to claim that Nazi references to American law were "simply attempts to cite vaguely relevant precedents for home-grown statutes and policies to deflect criticism" are simply wrong. Some Nazi writings can possibly be dismissed as efforts to "deflect criticism."[141] But Hitler was already praising America well before the Nazis took power; he could hardly have been aiming to counter bad press for a regime that did not yet exist. The same is true of Koellreutter. He published his book in German, a language that few foreigners found easily accessible (and, following customary Nazi practice, he published it in *Fraktur*, a script that foreigners without a strong command of German find irritatingly difficult to decipher). There is nothing propagandistic about the tenor of his text. There is no sign that Koellreutter's book, which would become a standard citation in Nazi Germany,[142] stirred any attention whatsoever abroad, and no good reason whatsoever for supposing that it was aimed at polishing Germany's international image. Koellreutter, as the leading German public lawyer, was engaged in a lawyerly study of a subject important to Nazi policy making in the dawning months of the "National Revolution." This was investigation of American immigration law by Nazis, for Nazis.

Much further investigation of the same kind took place over the following two years, as lawyers and bureaucrats wrestled with the political and doctrinal challenges in creating new citizenship and naturalization law. A few examples of how the legal literature described American law will give a sense of the interest in America in the German air of the early 1930s. I begin with the *National Socialist Handbook for Law and Legislation*. This was an immense tome published in the winter of 1934–35 under the editorship of Hans Frank, head of the Party Office for Legal Affairs, and later Governor-General and lord of the Nazi terror regime in occupied Poland. As its title indicates, the *National Socialist Handbook* was intended to mark out the path for future Nazi lawmaking. It included contributions on every aspect of the law, composed by various Nazi lawyers under Frank's direction. It is a point of some significance that the *Handbook* made special reference to the American model more than once:

National Socialist Handbook for Law and Legislation (1934–35):

The Law on the Revocation of Naturalization and the Withdrawal of German Citizenship of 1933 distinguishes between desirable and undesirable immigration. In this connection it is opportune to direct the reader's attention to the fact that the difference between desirable and undesirable naturalization has played an important role in the Immigration Law of the United States for some years.[143]

Particularly striking is the *Handbook* article on "*Volk*, Race and State." This was a basic review of how to craft race legislation for a new Nazi order, authored by Herbert Kier, at the time a junior academic at the University of Berlin and later one of Heinrich Himmler's operatives.[144] Kier devoted a full quarter of his text to the American model, reviewing the whole range of race law, including anti-miscegenation (which he described in state-by-state detail) and segregation. The very closing paragraph of his article was dedicated to American immigration law, and to hailing America as the forerunner of Nazism:

American immigration legislation shows that in the USA a clear understanding has been achieved that a unified North American *Volk* body can only emerge from the "melting pot" if wholly foreign racial population masses are not tossed in with the core population, which is English-Scandinavian-German in origin, and thus made up of racially related peoples. These two populations [i.e., the "core population" and the "wholly foreign racial population"] feel such natural antipathy that they resist being welded together. Once this fundamental recognition has been attained, it is only a matter of logical thinking to pay tribute to it in political ideology and above all in the creation of a concept of the *Volk*. National Socialism is the first to do this and the time will hopefully yet come when the *Völker* who are to be

numbered among the European cultural circle will acknowl-
edge this epochal deed, which called upon them to come to
their senses and remember their original and essential values.[145]

Thus the concluding words of the standard Nazi handbook chapter on how to craft race legislation. America had attained the "fundamental recognition" and taken the first steps; Nazi Germany was
carrying the logic rigorously forward; in time it was to be hoped
that all of the "European culture circle" would join in.

Many other texts can be adduced as well, all of them painting the
picture of a racist, and therefore attractive, American legal model—
though all of them also acknowledging that America had its flaws,
and many of them warning that Americans might yet backslide or
decay. America was described in the standard Nazi jargon as country founded in *Gemeinschaft*, the *Volk* community:

> Edgar Saebisch, *Der Begriff der Staatsangehörigkeit* (*The Concept
> of the "National"* [as opposed to the "Citizen"]) (1934):
>   America possesses a proud consciousness of *Gemeinschaft*.
> Any state, which like this one adopts a posture of fundamental
> rejection of would-be immigrants trying to push their way in,
> which subjects those immigrants whom it chooses to a series
> of tests and confessions of loyalty, shows that it values mem-
> bership in a *Gemeinschaft* as a precious good. This high level of
> self-esteem grows out of a profound national consciousness,
> which jealously guards its closed *Gemeinschaft* against new for-
> eign intruders.[146]

It was a country committed to "Nordic" supremacy:

> Martin Staemmler, *Rassenpflege im Völkischen Staat* (*The Main-
> tenance of Race Purity in the* Völkisch *State*) (1935):
>   That the Americans have begun to think about the mainte-
> nance of race purity, and thus to ask not only about eugenics,

but also about membership in individual races, can be seen in their immigration laws, which completely forbid the immigration of yellows, and place immigration from the individual European countries under sharp supervision, here principally admitting members of the decidedly Nordic peoples (English, German, Scandinavian states), whereas Southern and Eastern Europeans receive only a very weak portion of the admissions. The American knows very well who has made his land great. He sees that the Nordic blood is drying up, and seeks to refresh that blood through his immigration legislation.[147]

It was a country whose ruling whites were determined to keep foreign elements at bay:

Detlef Sahm, *Die Vereinigten Staaten von Amerika und das Problem der nationalen Einheit* (*The United States of America and the Problem of National Unity*) (1936):

The *legal and social position* of racial minorities as well as foreigners is evidence of the fact that large portions of the population do not belong to the dominant circles, and indeed stand in part in direct opposition to them. The circles of those who can trace their entry far back [in American history] try to protect their supremacy [*Oberherrschaft*] and to guarantee it for all future times. For that reason they focus their efforts on assimilating the foreign bodies into the nation through *education*, and *preventing the influx of racially foreign elements* [*artfremder Elemente*]. The Immigration and Naturalization Laws speak volumes about this effort.[148]

There are many such quotes: As one author put it, America was "sounding the loudest warning cry" about the "danger" of race-mixing; it had produced race-based immigration legislation from which all the "Nordic" world should learn; the issue was after all one of "life and death" for the white race.[149]

These were more than casual references to the "warning cries" sounded in American immigration law. The publications of the early 1930s included lengthy and carefully documented studies of American immigration law and jurisprudence. For example, Heinrich Krieger, a young Nazi lawyer who was the single most important figure in the Nazi assimilation of American race law, dedicated thirty-five well-informed and thoughtful pages to American immigration and naturalization law in his important 1936 book *Das Rassenrecht in den Vereinigten Staaten* (*Race Law in the United States*).[150] I will return to Krieger's book, and his biography, in more depth in Chapter 2.

Krieger was not alone. Another striking example of a Nazi closely engaging with American citizenship law is Johann von Leers. Leers was a leading so-called "Jew expert" involved in the earliest stages of the drafting process that led to the Nuremberg Laws.[151] He was one of the more repellant of Nazi lawyer/anti-Semites, with one of the stranger careers. A member of the party from an early date, Leers escaped Germany after the war, at first to Argentina. In the 1950s he moved to Egypt, where he became an advisor on anti-Israel propaganda to Gamal Abdel Nasser. Convinced that Christian Europe had abandoned the world-historical struggle against the Jews, Leers converted to Islam, dying in Egypt in 1965 as "Omar Amin."[152] In his 1936 book-length pamphlet *Blood and Race: A Tour through the History of Peoples*, Leers devoted twenty-three full pages to American race law. His review included not only an account of the Fourteenth Amendment, of Jim Crow segregation, and a state-by-state review of anti-miscegenation laws, but also thirteen pages on immigration and naturalization that included detailed statistics and discussion of the law with regard to each racial minority.[153]

Certain aspects of American immigration law attracted particular interest among Nazi lawyers. Authors were intrigued by the American treatment of naturalization and denaturalization. Edgar Saebisch, author of the 1934 study *The Concept of the "National,"* was

certainly something of a skeptic about the United States.[154] Nevertheless he pointed admiringly to certain American approaches to
naturalization. "The rigorous attitude of American law," he noted,
"reveals itself in the provisions created for wartime." Even before
the experience of World War I, the Americans, unlike the British
and the French, had passed wise legislation denying the right of
naturalization to citizens of any county with which America was
at war.[155] The same author also highlighted an American idea of
particular interest for the history of the Nuremberg Laws. This was
an idea found in the Cable Act of 1922, which concerned the citizenship of married women. Historically the citizenship of wives in
the Western world was subsumed in that of their husbands. But
by the beginning of the twentieth century modern systems were
generally rejecting that doctrine, and the Cable Act was one of a
number of statutes in various countries that abrogated the historic
rule. Unlike statutes elsewhere, however, the Cable Act included
a race-based exception: until 1930, the act made a point of strip-
ping American women of their citizenship if they were misguided
enough to marry noncitizen Asian men.[156] Saebisch, unaware that
that provision of the Cable Act had been repealed, saluted it as a
healthy example of legislation motivated by race consciousness: "If
an American woman marries a Japanese man, then she does not
retain her citizenship, as she would if she contracted other foreign
marriages, but loses it upon marriage. This consequence is obviously meant as the well-deserved punishment for the female citizen
who enters into a union with a person incapable of forming part of
the *Gemeinschaft*."[157] This sort of race rule, expelling women who
had polluted themselves through marriage to a "foreign body," was
of great interest to Nazi writers. Leers identified a similar example
from the Anglo-American world in his *Blood and Race*: "If a woman
of English nationality and Christian faith marries a Mohammedan
who is not a British citizen, but perhaps a subject or citizen of a
Mohammedan state, she loses her British nationality as a result of

her marriage, and if the husband and wife take up residence in a Mohammedan land that is neither a possession nor a protectorate of His Britannic Majesty, they fall under subjection to Mohammedan law."[158] What reader could have guessed that Leers himself would himself die as the "Mohammedan" Omar Amin in a "Mohammedan land" thirty years later? At any rate, Anglo-American practices of denaturalization upon marriage seemed to merit serious attention from Nazi policy makers. And as we shall see, they were practices that bore some relation to an important aspect of the Nuremberg Laws. The implementation of the Nuremberg Laws focused in a similar way on marital choices: the Nazis faced the question of which half-Jewish *Mischlinge*, "mongrels," would count as "Jews" by law. The answer they gave, in part, was that "mongrels" were "Jews" if they chose to marry other "Jews," thus revealing their Jewish "inclinations"[159] or the "strength" of their "Jewish blood."[160] Like an American woman who took a Japanese spouse, these were individuals who had chosen to associate themselves with a foreign element abhorrent to the healthy *Volk*-community.

THE NAZIS LOOK TO AMERICAN SECOND-CLASS CITIZENSHIP

American immigration law featured especially frequently in the Nazi legal literature, perhaps because Hitler himself had praised it so demonstratively. But Nazi authors did not neglect American citizenship law, with its creation of de jure and de facto forms of second-class citizenship for blacks, Puerto Ricans, Filipinos, Chinese, and Native Americans. As Mazower rightly guesses, this was indeed a topic of special interest in the Nazi Germany of the Second Nuremberg Law.

Nazi authors of the 1930s remained especially intrigued by the de facto legal degradation of American blacks, whose citizenship they, like their German predecessors, knew to be a "dead letter."[161]

In fact, the topic of black disenfranchisement in the United States seemed of sufficient political interest that it made its way into mass-circulation party publications. For example a cheap party magazine, intended for a broad Nazi readership, the *SA-Führer*, reported on the meaninglessness of black citizenship in the United States.[162] So did a particularly interesting 1936 article, published in *Neues Volk* ("New *Volk*"), a propaganda newsletter produced by the National Socialist Office on Racial Policy. This striking piece of party race propaganda, which promised to explain "White and Black in America" to the general German population, opened with a handy map of the forty-eight states, showing the precise status of American disenfranchisement and miscegenation law throughout the country under the heading "Statutory Restrictions on Negro Rights." The article then proceeded with a breezy account of black life and history in the United States, accompanied by seven pages of photos. It focused particularly on New York City. New York blacks, it informed its readers, maintained their own culture in Harlem by night; but by day they commuted downtown, to serve as "shoe-shine boys and elevator operators, gleaming like patent leather and with kinky hair like lamb's wool." (Some of the blacks worked as waiters in New York as well, the article reported, but "they are not allowed to speak a word to the white guests, and bring them the menu on a tray, not in their hand.")

Like other Nazi literature, this article, which carried the title "How Race Questions Arise," warned that the Negro problem represented a grave threat to America. In particular, it noted rising black birthrates, while its illustrations included reproductions of advertisements for skin-lightening cream and hair-straightening pomade—products that blacks might use to disguise their "gleaming" skin and "lamb's-wool" hair in order to penetrate white society. Nevertheless, the article emphasized that Americans were taking healthy measures to combat the race danger that they faced, just as Nazis

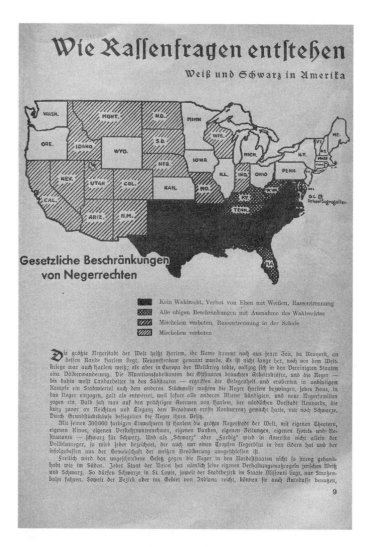

Figure 3. "'How Race Questions Arise.' A Map of the 48 States Showing 'Statutory Restrictions on Negro Rights.'" *Source*: *Neues Volk. Blätter des Rassenpolitischen Amtes der NSDAP* 4, no. 3 (1936): 9. Courtesy of the University of Michigan Library.

Figure 4. Images from the lives of American Blacks: Clockwise from top: "Shoeshine Boys in America Are Exclusively Negroes." "The Black World Metropolis: The Neighborhood of Harlem in the Northern New York Is Populated Only by Coloreds." "Mongrels Too Are Reckoned among the Coloreds." *Source*: *Neues Volk. Blätter des Rassenpolitischen Amtes der NSDAP* 4, no. 3 (1936): 13. Courtesy of the University of Michigan Library.

Figure 5. Images from the lives of American Blacks. At top: "Young Negro boys in Harlem. The Negroes are multiplying significantly more strongly than the white population of the United States. Their constantly growing numbers are a source of great concern to American statesmen." *Source*: *Neues Volk. Blätter des Rassenpolitischen Amtes der NSDAP* 4, no. 3 (1936): 14. Courtesy of the University of Michigan Library.

Figure 6. "Mixed marriages between White and Black are forbidden in most states of the Union. The former Negro boxer and world champion Jack Johnson cannot return to America, because he married a white woman in Paris." *Source: Neues Volk. Blätter des Rassenpolitischen Amtes der NSDAP* 4, no. 3 (1936): 15. Courtesy of the University of Michigan Library.

were doing, even if "a certain part" of the American press was hostile to National Socialism: "The United States too [just like Nazi Germany] has racist politics and policies. What is lynch justice, if not the natural resistance of the *Volk* to an alien race that is attempting to gain the upper hand? Most states of the Union have special laws directed against the Negroes, which limit their voting rights, freedom of movement, and career possibilities. For a while, there was a plan to create a Negro reservation in the Southern states, similar to the Indian reservations."[163] There is no way of guessing where the authors of the article picked up the odd notion that America had planned a "Negro reservation." South Africa had such reservations, as Leers observed;[164] but the United States did not. In any case, the article shows that in 1936, as the Nuremberg Laws took hold, Nazi Party officials were making an effort to publicize the American method of creating de facto second-class citizenship to average Germans on the street, at a time when Germany too was subjecting its Jews to "racist politics and policy." This was propaganda, but it was propaganda directed at the home population, not at foreign critics.[165]

Meanwhile the technical legal literature continued to explicate the law of American second-class citizenship, just as the German literature had done in earlier decades. The United States, a 1933 book reported, had invented for its subject populations a novel, intermediate category between citizenship and statelessness, an unprecedented form of legal "limbo." This novel category covered not only blacks, but also the subject populations of Filipinos and Puerto Ricans.[166] Krieger, in a much-cited 1934 article that (as we shall see) would be influential on the internal deliberations over the drafting of the Blood Law, pointed out that not only Blacks, but also Chinese were deprived of meaningful voting rights in the United States.[167] *Deutsche Justiz*, a leading party organ on legal affairs, highlighted the same fact.[168] "The Negroes are *not* equal before the law," wrote one author in a 1935 book touting John C. Calhoun as a racist inspiration for Germany; and they could never be made equal, because "full political equality would obviously put an end to the sexual separation between the races—and the healthy race instinct of the Anglo-Saxons has so far rejected that."[169]

It is particularly noteworthy that Nazi authors of the early 1930s saw clear parallels between the American "Negro problem" and their own "Jewish problem"; it is simply false to assert, as scholars have done, that America was of no interest to Nazi Germany because the Jews were not expressly persecuted there. For example, the same admirer of John C. Calhoun judged that the only desperate hope of America lay in mass deportation of the blacks—just as the only desperate hope of the Germans lay in the Zionist movement.[170]

More importantly, the technical legal literature saw the same parallels. From the point of view of Nazi lawyers in the early 1930s, the Jewish problem that Germany faced was first and foremost a problem of Jewish "influence," particularly in government, bureaucracy, and law.[171] It was for that reason that the Party Program of 1920 included its Point 6:

> 6. Only a citizen is permitted the right to decide on the leadership [*Führung*] and laws of the state. Therefore we demand that every public office, regardless of what kind, regardless of whether it is an office of the Reich, of the constituent States of the Reich, or any municipality, be accessible only to citizens.

It was for the same reason that the earliest Nazi anti-Jewish legislation set out to exclude Jews from government, universities, and the legal profession.[172] And when Nazi lawyers considered the American deprivation of black rights, they saw, bizarrely, a precisely parallel effort to combat black "influence." For them, American blacks were not a desperately oppressed and impoverished population, but a menacing "alien race" of invaders that threatened to get "the upper hand," and therefore had to be thwarted. (This lunatic view, it should be said, was one that Nazis shared with American racists.)[173] Krieger's influential 1934 article explained that it was because the "ruling race" in America had to work to prevent black "influence" that American lawyers had developed covert legal subterfuges to deprive the black population of full political rights despite their notional constitutionally guaranteed citizenship.[174] The article went into considerable detail about how these subterfuges functioned,[175] and expressed cautious optimism that America would eventually move toward a more "open" form of legal racism, of the kind being developed at home in Germany.[176] Sahm similarly surveyed the techniques of the deprivation of black political rights, which were designed "to depress *the political influence of the Negroes to a minimum*" in the southern states.[177] Germans saw the same issues in the status of American Jews: thus Sahm explained that American Jews, while technically suffering no legal disabilities, were relegated to a "subordinate social position" through nonlegal means such as university quotas; the respectable legal profession in particular remained closed to them.[178] In this manner the United States was working to keep its Jews at bay without formally abrogating their constitutional protections. (Leers thought the same thing, though he was sure that mere custom was inadequate to stave off the dangers posed by Jews; formal law was needed.)[179]

Sahm is a particularly noteworthy author, since he put special care into examining American law in ways that brought out its resemblances to the new law of the Reich. Hitler had written in *Mein Kampf* that "the *völkisch* state divides its inhabitants into three classes: Staatsbürger (citizens), Staatsangehörige (nationals) and

Ausländer (aliens)."[180] Sahm, without citing the Führer expressly, explained to his German readers that American law followed the canonical *Mein Kampf* model precisely:

American public law distinguishes between Staatsbürger (citizens), Staatsangehörige (nationals) and Ausländer (aliens).

Staatsbürgerschaft ("Citizenship") is the highest legal level. One becomes an American citizen by birth or through naturalization. . . .

Alongside the citizens there are also nationals who do not enjoy the rights of citizenship: "*non-citizen nationals.*" Such nationals include most inhabitants of the Philippines, while inhabitants of Hawaii, Porto Rico, the Virgin Islands also possess American citizenship.[181]

The Nuremberg Laws declared that only citizens enjoyed "full political rights." American law, Sahm observed, had a parallel rule, distinguishing between "political rights" and "civil rights."[182] Sahm emphasized that American law further guaranteed that certain groups who technically possessed "political" rights were nevertheless excluded from voting: the disfavored groups included not only blacks but also Native Americans.[183] As for aliens, they faced a variety of disabilities under American law—a matter of natural interest to the Nazis, who since 1920 had been insisting that foreigners must benefit only from limited "guest right."[184] By such means the Americans, as Drascher wrote in his *Supremacy of the White Race*, "took care to guarantee that the decisive positions in the leadership [*Führung*] of the state would be kept in the hands of Anglo-Saxons alone."[185]

Once again it was not only the Nazis who found these American developments fascinating. Throughout Europe it was a commonplace in the 1930s and 1940s that the South, through its systematic deprivation of the voting rights of blacks (and Mexicans and Native Americans),[186] had embarked on the creation of something that looked unmistakably like the American version of a race-based fascist order. "The Ku Klux Klan are the fascists of America," a French author reported; they were a group founded in order to combat black enfranchisement.[187] Bertram Schrieke, a Dutch ethnographer who published an interesting book on American race relations in 1936, declared that the southern "process of undoing reconstruction—with its violence, intimidation, open bribery, stuffing ballot boxes, manipulation and falsification of election returns, use of tissue ballots etc., all serving to eliminate Negro voters ... reminds one strongly of the rise of the Nazis in Germany";[188] "[o]n account of its one-party system and the precarious state of civil liberties," wrote Gunnar Myrdal in 1944, "the South is sometimes referred to as fascist."[189] Nevertheless, if Europeans widely shared this thought, it is especially striking to discover Nazis themselves expressing it—declaring, as Krieger did, that the Democratic Party of the South, through its "racist election law," had built a one-party system, and that the only remaining question was whether it would succeed, as the Nazis had done, in making "the Party an organ of the State."[190]

CONCLUSION

All this Nazi lionization of white supremacy in America, and all this Nazi rummaging in American immigration and citizenship law, requires some careful assessment, and some careful choice of words. The Nazis were clearly deeply interested in the American example, but it would be a mistake to draw overblown conclusions about the direct influence of the American model on the Citizenship Law. There was never any possibility that the Nazis would copy the Citizenship Law directly from what they found in American parallels, no matter how much they praised them. America may have been the global leader in the creation of racist law, well known and much cited long before Hitler came to power; but as the Nazis regularly observed, American law was not open about its racist goals, at least when it came to citizenship and immigration. (We shall see in the next chapter that American anti-miscegenation law was quite different.) In their citizenship and immigration law, Americans had to work around the requirements of the Fourteenth Amendment, and more broadly around their announced traditions of equality; and in consequence their law was a law of covert devices and legal subterfuges. American law, as Krieger wrote, was a law of *Umwege*, devious legal pathways. The Nazis certainly found this American juristic mischief engaging, and they were glad for the chance to point out the depth of American legal racism, both in party propaganda and in the technical legal literature. But for their part they fully intended to create an open system of racist citizenship, and if for no other reason than that they had no need to borrow from the letter of American law. Nazi race law was not going to be a law of national quotas, poll taxes, grandfather clauses, or literacy tests.

In any case, it is inherently unlikely that we would discover unmodified borrowing. Nazi jurists were German lawyers, the representatives of a deep and proud juristic tradition, one that generally exported law to other countries, not one that mechanically borrowed. What is more, they were German lawyers who were convinced that they were participating in a "National Revolution" that represented a breakthrough in human history. It would be surprising indeed if these men had simply aped American law, and they did not do so.

So it would be wrong to say that the Nazis directly "borrowed" from the Americans in the making of the Citizenship Law. This is not a story of what, in the jargon of comparative law, would be called an American "transplant" into Nazi Germany.

At the same time, it would be foolish and craven to minimize Nazi interest in what American law represented. From *Mein Kampf* on the Nazis did indeed lionize American white supremacy and did indeed rummage in American immigration and citizenship law. The *National Socialist Handbook* did indeed describe America as the country that had achieved the "fundamental recognition" of the historic racist mission that Nazi Germany was now called to fulfill. In that sense the legal literature was entirely in tune with the historical literature that announced that until the coming of Hitler the United States had held "the leadership of the white peoples" in the "Aryan struggle for world domination." If Nazi legal authors believed that American race legislation was highly "imperfect" and therefore deserving of reproach,[191] if they derided the activities of New York Jews like Louis Brodsky, they nevertheless thought of the United States as a country groping its way toward the policies of a healthy *völkisch* order, in obedience to the healthy American race consciousness[192]—as the country that had, in the view of *Mein Kampf*, taken the first steps.

So if there was no direct borrowing from America in the Citizenship Law, there was nevertheless something whose importance for the mentality of Nazi lawyers and policy makers should not be dismissed. In immigration and citizenship the American example served not so much as a direct template, but as welcome evidence that "race consciousness" had already begun to shape the law in a leading "Nordic" polity. But it *did* serve as welcome evidence, and it would be wrong to underestimate the importance of that fact. American law offered the Nazis something that matters a great deal to modern lawyers: it offered them confirmation that the winds of history were blowing in their direction. Their America was what Hitler described it to be: a dynamic country whose race consciousness had stirred the first substantial moves toward the sort of race order that it was Germany's mission to bring to full fruition. Comparative law influence is not just a matter of lifting particular regulations, copying particular paragraphs, or transplanting particular institutions. Lawyers, even Nazi lawyers, need a sense of the propriety and necessity of their law, and the presence of foreign parallels can provide salutary comfort and inspiration. Modern lawyers in particular often want to believe that they are soldiering toward a better future—and evidence that other countries are soldiering toward the same better future, in however bumbling a way, matters to them. This is perhaps especially true of lawyers plunged into a self-consciously revolutionary situation.

And painful though it may be for us to admit it, it is not surprising that these lawyer-participants in the Nazi "National Revolution," like far right-wingers before them, seized on the American example. American race-based immigration and citizenship law did in fact set the standard in the early twentieth century. The Nazi case suggests how much truth there is in the verdict that the United States was "the leader in developing explicitly racist policies of nationality and immigration."[193] This was a realm in which the creative legal culture of the United States set the international tone in the early twentieth century, much as it sets the tone in areas like corporate law today. That is why even Nazi Germany looked to America.

Still, what we discover in the making of the Citizenship Law cannot rightly be called "borrowing." If we are to hunt for more provocative evidence of something that looks more like borrowing, we must turn to its companion measure, the Blood Law.

CHAPTER 2

PROTECTING NAZI BLOOD
AND NAZI HONOR

Dr. Möbius: I am reminded of something an American said to us recently. He explained, "We do the same thing you are doing. But why do you have to say it so explicitly in your laws?"

State Secretary Freisler: But the Americans put it in their own laws even more explicitly!

—*June 5, 1934*

When we turn to the Blood Law, we enter a world of what refugees from Nazi Germany decried as *Rassenwahn*, "race madness"[1]—of Nazi ravings about the Jewish menace, and fanatical Nazi obsessions with the state enforcement of racial and sexual purity and the criminalization and expulsion of those who endangered it. The Blood Law, with its ban on race mixing in sex and marriage, would be condemned by postwar European lawyers as the epitome of the violation of natural rights,[2] but in the Nazi period the Supreme Court of the Reich declared it to be nothing less than a "fundamental constitutional law of the national socialist state."[3] Nazi lawyers presented it to the public as an essential measure for maintaining a German race that was "pure and unmixed";[4] as the basic commentary on the Nuremberg Laws proclaimed, the Blood Law, like the Citizenship Law, was imperatively necessary in order to prevent "any further penetration of Jewish blood into the body of the German *Volk*,"[5] and the rhetoric surrounding it was shrill with warnings about the dangers of sexual contact with Jews.

"Mixing" was the term that Nazi writers constantly used to describe the menace of such "penetration of Jewish blood into the body of German *Volk*," evoked by a variety of words based on the German root *-misch*, "mix." Sick societies were societies that had witnessed the "mixing" (*Vermischung*) of *Völker*; what such mixing yielded, the Nazi literature often said, was a degenerate racial *Mischmasch*, a "mishmash." The aim of the Nuremberg Laws was to safeguard Germany from such degeneration, making it "forever impossible for Jewdom to mix itself [*Vermischung*] with the German *Volk*," and the key legal terminology was based on the same root: What the Blood Law aimed to prohibit was a *Mischehe* or *Mischheirat*, "mixed marriage." What sexual mixing threatened to spawn, not least, was a degenerate *Mischling* child—a "mixed one," a "mongrel."

In the effort to capture the obsessive anti-mixing sensibility that lay behind the Blood Law, it is useful to draw on the pronouncements of two especially intriguing Nazi figures: Helmut Nicolai, who made himself "the leading Party legal philosopher" in the early 1930s,[6] and Achim Gercke, a specialist on "racial prophylaxis" who served in the Ministry of the Interior and was responsible for an early draft of the statute and much later policy making.[7] Both men were prominent in the early years of Nazi rule; both would be purged in 1935 on the same charge: homosexuality.[8] We cannot know whether the charge was true—whether these Nazi fanatics of sexual purity were indeed homosexual men, many of whose neighbors could well have viewed them with sexual disgust. In any case, the two were at the forefront in the early 1930s, and their speeches and writings illustrate the mentality of the Nazi fanaticism about the dangers of sexual mixing that informed the crafting of the Blood Law.

Nicolai and Gercke preached fervently against what Nazis called the crime of *Rassenschande*, "race defilement"—sexual unions between Germans (especially German women) and racial inferiors (especially Jewish men.)[9] The general populace, Nazi leaders fretted, simply did not grasp the monstrosity of sexual congress between Germans and Jews, which endangered the entire race; Germans had to be "educated and enlightened";[10] they had to be, as it were, converted. To that end Gercke, for example, gave a radio lecture in the summer of 1933 with the memorable title "Learning to Think Like a Racist." He patiently explained to his listeners, still in need of Nazi indoctrination, that marriage with a Jew was simply "sick."[11] Nicolai for his part, in a pamphlet published in 1932, the frightening year before Hitler's installation as Chancellor, was at pains to explain to voters that Jews were vectors of mongrelization: Indeed they were not, properly speaking, members of a "pure" race at all: they were all *Mischlinge*, all mongrels, the products of thousands of years of heedless interbreeding.[12]

Nicolai's 1932 warnings about the dangers posed by Jewish mongrels rested on the standard wild-eyed Nazi view of history, much repeated in the literature of the time. Human history was a millennia-long chronicle of race decay—of superior races that had degenerated, and eventually been completely submerged, as a result of race mixing. With "Nordic" Germany at risk, it was urgent that there be new marriage legislation. Race mixing through indiscriminate marriage was akin to race mixing through indiscriminate immigration, and the Jews were agents of pollution in both respects:

Today the different *Völker* are essentially kept separate by international borders. The fact that so far no stronger mixing [*Vermischung*] of all *Völker* has taken place than what has occurred, that therefore the *Völker* are racially distinguished from each at all, has to do strictly with the sedentariness of most *Völker*. That sedentariness does not exist with the Jews. It is true that they maintain their own *völkisch* unity through the strictest possible closure of the community, supported by the Jewish religion. Nevertheless they have always been nomads, and they are still nomads today. It corresponds to their sensibility and their sense of justice that state borders should be allowed to vanish and that all the ties that unite a *völkisch* community should be loosened, that the various *Völker* should mix with each other promiscuously and create a single unified humanity.[13]

Jews were "foreign bodies" who violated both international and sexual boundaries; they opened the door to the worst of possible futures, the emergence of "a single unified humanity." "Our *Volk* is in danger!," as another Nazi legal text cried in 1934, repeating the standard slogan.[14]

One might wish that all this Nazi raving were remote from anything to be found in the United States. But in fact, as this chapter shows, it is with the Blood Law that we discover the most provocative evidence of direct Nazi engagement with American legal models, and the most unsettling signs of direct influence. American law was expressly invoked in the key radical Nazi document establishing the initial framework for the Blood Law, the so-called *Preußische Denkschrift*, the Prussian Memorandum, circulated by Nazi radicals in 1933. In the subsequent debates—in particular in an important June 1934 planning meeting preserved in a lengthy stenographic transcript—American models were regularly discussed. In particular, American models were championed by the most radical Nazi faction, the fiercest advocates of a stringent ban on sexual mixing. Finally the Blood Law itself that emerged at Nuremberg bore the marks, as I shall argue, of American influence.

The story of American influence that this chapter has to tell is certainly depressing. But it may come, once again, as no great surprise to readers knowledgeable about early twentieth-century American race history. It is a familiar fact that much of America was infected with the same race madness: as the Nazi literature noted, there were plenty of Americans who simply "knew" that black men regularly raped white women.[15] American courts, as German authors were aware, were capable of delivering matter-of-fact holdings such as "the mixing of the two races would create a mongrel population and a degraded civilization";[16] the American Supreme Court entertained briefs from southern states whose arguments were indistinguishable from those of the Nazis;[17] and southern racists like Senator Theodore Bilbo, staunch supporter of the New Deal in the early 1930s, could tell tales of the decay of races through mixing every bit as wild-eyed as Helmut Nicolai's: "Pleading against 'mongrelization' in the anti-lynching debate of 1938, a process he claimed had destroyed white civilization over much of the globe, Bilbo took a page from Hitler's *Mein Kampf* to assert that merely 'one drop of Negro blood placed in the veins of the purest Caucasian destroys the inventive genius of his mind and palsies his creative faculty.' "[18] (In fact, Bilbo was going further than the Nazis were willing to go: as we shall see, the Nazis firmly rejected the one-drop rule as too extreme.)

Nevertheless, if America too was infected with race madness, what made the United States influential on the Blood Law was not its race madness, but the distinctive legal techniques that Americans had developed to combat the menace of race mixing. Here once again, America was the global leader.

First and foremost, the United States offered *the* model of anti-miscegenation legislation. The notion that marriage between "superior" and "inferior" races should be avoided was widespread in the world in the age of early twentieth-century eugenics.[19] Nevertheless actual legislative bans were a rarity; certainly the Nazis had a hard time uncovering non-American examples. As Reich Minister of Justice Gürtner declared at the June 1934 planning meeting that will occupy much of this chapter, it was "naturally very attractive to look around in the world to see how this problem has been attacked by other *Völker*," and the United States provided the only model that the Justice Ministry found to exploit.[20] The same was true of the published Nazi literature, which identified many instances of customary or socially enforced prohibitions, but few statutes outside the United States.[21]

It is especially significant that the United States offered examples of an exceptional legislative practice: not only did thirty American states declare racially mixed marriages civilly invalid, many of them also threatened those who entered into such marriages with punishment, sometimes harsh. This was highly unusual. Criminalization of marriage is rare in legal history. Many species of marriage have been deemed invalid over the centuries, but the only form regularly criminalized and prosecuted in the modern Western world has been bigamy.[22] Even a thoroughly race-obsessed country like Australia in the era of the "White Australia" policy did not follow America's menacing lead. A principal Australian law of 1910, for example, simply decreed that "[n]o marriage of a female aboriginal with any person other than an aboriginal shall be celebrated without the permission, in writing, of a Protector authorized by the Minister to grant permission in such cases."[23] The statute did in principle allow for prosecution, but it did not suggest that violators would face severe punishment.[24] The contrast with the anti-miscegenation statute of an

American state like Maryland was stark. The Maryland statute was far more detailed in its discussion of who counted as a member of which race, and harsh indeed in its threats:

> All marriages between a white person and a Negro, or between a white person and a person of Negro descent, to the third generation, inclusive, or between a white person and a member of the Malay race or between a Negro and a member of the Malay race, or between a person of Negro descent, to the third generation, inclusive, and a member of the Malay race, or between a person of Negro descent, to the third generation, inclusive, and a member of the Malay race or between a Negro and a member of the Malay race, or between a person of Negro descent, to the third generation, inclusive, and a member of the Malay race, are forever prohibited, and shall be void; *and any person violating the provisions of this Section shall be deemed guilty of an infamous crime, and be punished by imprisonment in the penitentiary for not less than eighteen months nor more than ten years.*[25]

Draconian penalization of this kind represented a sort of law that only the United States had to offer. The only other even partially comparable example that the Nazi literature highlighted in the early 1930s was found in South Africa, which penalized extramarital sex between the races, but not marriage.[26] As we shall see, the notion that racial miscegenation could be punished criminally was deeply appealing to Nazis like Nicolai, Gercke, and the radical Nazi lawyers who drafted the Prussian Memorandum of 1933; it is in the criminalization of racially mixed marriage that we see the strongest signs of direct American influence on the Nuremberg laws.

American anti-miscegenation law had something else to offer as well: law on how to classify "mongrels"—what I will call "mongrelization law." The Nazi faced far-reaching problems in the treatment of the mongrels of Germany as they set out to combat race mixing. A majority of German Jews were incontestably Jews. But the German Jewry had a substantial history of intermarriage, and there was also a heavy proportion of mixed-descent persons whose status was uncertain. By the official Nazi reckoning in 1935 there were 550,000 full and three-quarter Jews, 200,000 half Jews, and 100,000 quarter Jews in Germany.[27] How much Jewish blood was enough to indelibly taint a child of part "Aryan" descent? Which mongrelized German nationals would fall under the axe of the new Nazi laws? Here again, as German authors observed, the United States had basic lessons to teach: because it had a long history of sexual relations between masters and slaves, it was a country, as Eduard Meyer reported in 1920, that was groaning under the weight of "an enormous mass of mongrels,"[28] and it had consequently developed a large body of law on mongrelization, defining who did and did not belong to which race. Unlike American immigration and citizenship law, moreover, this law was "open": it made no secret of its racist aims, and employed no devious pathways or subterfuges.

American mongrelization law represented, once again, the only body of foreign jurisprudence offering an extensive corpus of doctrine that Nazi policy makers found to investigate and exploit, and exploit it they did. But here we arrive at the most uncomfortable irony in this history: when it came to the law of mongrelization the Nazis were not ready to import American law wholesale. This is not, however, because they found American law too enlightened or egalitarian. The painful paradox, as we shall see, is that Nazis lawyers, even radical ones, found American law on mongrelization too harsh to be embraced by the Third Reich. From the Nazi point of view this was a domain in which American race law simply went too far for Germany to follow. Nevertheless, we shall also see that Nazi lawyers put real effort into studying the law of the American states, in the search for what wisdom they had to provide.

TOWARD THE BLOOD LAW: BATTLES IN THE STREETS AND THE MINISTRIES

Before turning to the details of what Nazi policy makers made of American miscegenation and mongrelization law, it is important once again to provide some historical context. Nazi investigation of American anti-miscegenation legislation took place against the background of several conflicts that developed in the months after Hitler took power in early 1933. First, there was political conflict between street radicals, who wanted to carry the Nazi program forward through spontaneous pogrom-like violence, and party officials who wanted to keep control of the "National Revolution" in the hands of the state. Second, there was ongoing bureaucratic conflict between two groups: on the one hand Nazi radicals, who pushed for the harshest conceivable measures, and on the other hand lawyers of a more traditional bent, who tried to hew to older juristic conventions to the extent possible, and to bring some moderation to the Nazi ordinances and enactments. Finally, there was conflict over foreign relations. Radical Nazi plans to pass legislation disfavoring "colored" races met with angry protests from many parts of the world, including Japan, India, and South America.[29] Faced with the threat of boycotts, Nazi policy makers felt pressure to tone their racist legislative program down. All of these conflicts colored the history of the Nazi use of American law on marriage and sexual mixing.

BATTLES IN THE STREETS: THE CALL FOR "UNAMBIGUOUS LAWS"

Political conflict in the streets lay in the immediate background of the Nuremberg Laws. As historians have shown, the Nuremberg

Laws were promulgated in response to radical street violence. In 1933 and again in 1935, during the chaotic early years of the "National Revolution," there was widespread violence "from below"—what the Nazis called "individual actions" against Jews, many but not all fatal, that had not been sanctioned or directed by the authorities in Berlin.[30] These were incidents, inevitably, that sometimes particularly targeted cases of *Rassenschande*, "race-defiling" instances in which Jews were accused of engaging in sexual "mixing" with Germans.[31] Heinrich Krieger, the leading Nazi student of American race law, regarded these "individual actions" on the street as the German parallels to American lynch justice: just as inhabitants of the American South, motivated by their "race consciousness," acted outside legal channels to engage in deplorably wild and unregulated violence against black "race defilers," so too were Germans engaging in wild and unregulated violence against Jews[32]—"rising up," in the words of the Party Office on Race Policy, against "an alien race that [was] attempting to gain the upper hand."

The central Nazi leadership too viewed these "individual actions" as deplorable, for two reasons. First, they made for bad foreign press. Finance Minister Hjalmar Schacht was particularly concerned that street violence was damaging Germany's international image, and therefore impeding economic recovery, and he pushed hard for a crackdown.[33] Second, the "individual actions" reflected a breakdown in the central party control of affairs that was always integral to the Nazi ambitions. The Nazis favored official, orderly, and properly supervised state-sponsored persecution, not street-level lynchings or "actions" incited by low-level party members. As Gunnar Myrdal remarked in 1944, Nazi racists, unlike the racists in the American South, understood persecution to be the task for "the centralized organization of a fascist state,"[34] and popular lynch justice did not fit in.

It was such concerns about the dangers of German street violence that led to the promulgation of the Citizenship Law and

Blood Law at Nuremberg. Concerned that the "National Revolution" might slip out of control, the party set out to calm matters by creating "unambiguous laws" that would put the business of persecution securely in the hands of the state.[35] Over the months leading up to the "Party Rally of Freedom" in September 1935, Interior Minister Frick and others regularly declared that both citizenship and sex legislation was in preparation, precisely in the effort to bring order to the streets.[36]

BATTLES IN THE MINISTRIES: THE PRUSSIAN MEMORANDUM AND THE AMERICAN EXAMPLE

The preparation of the necessary "unambiguous laws" was, however, shadowed by bureaucratic conflict between Nazi radicals and more traditionally minded lawyers. Nazi Party radicals demanded far-reaching criminalization of sexual mixing. As early as 1930 Nazi deputies in the Reichstag had put forward a proposal to criminalize racially mixed marriage,[37] and after the party took power in 1933 radicals continued to press the same demand for the prevention of "any further penetration of Jewish blood into the body of the German *Volk*." Conventional lawyers, however, mounted considerable, and for a while successful, resistance. This conflict between Nazi radicals and conventional lawyers makes for a remarkable story, and it deserves some close attention. It is a major episode in modern legal history—a test case for how legal traditions could operate to impose limits during the descent into Nazism. And from the beginning, it was a conflict turned in part on the usefulness of the American model.

The radical program for the Nazification of German criminal law was laid out in the key text known as the Prussian Memorandum, first circulated in September 1933, at a moment when a wave of summer street violence had died down.[38] This hardline text, which established the basic terms for what would become the Blood Law two years later,[39] was composed by a team assembled by Hanns Kerrl, a Nazi radical who served as Prussian Minister of Justice. Kerrl's team was headed by Roland Freisler, a man who will loom large in this chapter. Freisler was an infamous Nazi lawyer, who would later serve as the President of the bloody Nazi People's Court—a "murderer in the service of Hitler," as one biographer calls him[40]—and attend the Wannsee Conference that decided on the extermination of the Jews.[41]

The main aim of the Prussian Memorandum on which Freisler and other radicals collaborated was to do away with the "liberal" criminal law of the Weimar Republic in favor of the harsh new approach typical of Nazi politics. To that end it detailed a list of demands for toughening criminal law that met with considerable critique from conventionally trained lawyers.[42] And among those demands was a passage that laid out the program that would be incorporated in the Blood Law two years later. That passage pointed to two examples for the new Nazi order to follow: medieval expulsions of the Jews in Europe—and modern-day American Jim Crow.

In this passage, which would be hotly debated both domestically and internationally, the authors of the Prussian Memorandum called for the creation of the three new race crimes of "Race Treason," "Causing Harm to the Honor of the Race," and "Race Endangerment." The authors began with a prologue invoking the Nazi view of history:

History teaches that racial disintegration [*Rassenzersetzung*] leads to the decline and fall of *Völker*. By contrast *Völker* that have rid themselves of racially foreign segments of the *Volk*, in particular of Jews, have blossomed (e.g., France after the expulsion of the Jews in the year 1394, England after their expulsion in the year 1291). . . . The fundamental principle of the egoistic age of the past, that everyone who bears a human countenance is equal, destroys the race and therewith the life force of the *Volk*. It is therefore the task of the National Socialist state to check the race-mixing that has been underway in Germany over the course of the centuries, and strive toward the goal of guaranteeing that Nordic blood, which is still determinative in the German people, should put its distinctive stamp on our life again.

In order to achieve these goals, the criminalization of racially mixed marriage was a burning necessity. Nevertheless the Memorandum held that existing mixed marriages were not to be disturbed:

> The first necessary condition for this so-called "Nordic-i-fication" [*Aufnordung*] is that henceforth no Jews, Negroes, or other coloreds, be absorbed into German blood. *The criminal prohibition of mixing* is to be so framed, that mixing between members of foreign blood communities or races, whose strict separation from German blood is to be determined by law, will be forbidden. It follows that the proscription will have no application to currently existing mixed marriages. *The future formation of mixed marriages shall be prevented by a law of the Reich.*

Leaving existing interracial marriages intact would indeed remain Nazi policy—though the party worked hard to encourage "Aryan" spouses to divorce their partners.[43] The Memorandum then proposed the creation of a new crime of "race treason":

Race Treason

> Every form of sexual mixing between a German and a member of a foreign race is to be punished as *race treason*, and indeed both parties are to be subject to punishment. . . .

Particularly deserving of punishment is the case in which sexual intercourse or marriage is induced through malicious deception.... As a matter of civil law, it must be declared that the fact that a marriage is mixed is grounds for its dissolution.

The Memorandum next turned to "Causing Harm to the Honor of the Race." This was the proposal, soon so controversial, that targeted "colored" races, thereby giving diplomatic offense to East Asians, South Asians, and South Americans. It was also the proposal that included the first of the many invocations of the United States that we shall examine in this chapter:

Causing Harm to the Honor of the Race

Causing harm to the honor of the race must also be made criminally punishable. It scandalously flouts the sentiments of the *Volk* when, for example, German women shamelessly consort with Negroes. That said, the provision is to be limited to cases in which the association takes place in public and occurs in a shameless manner and gives gross offense to the sentiments of the *Volk* (for example indecent dancing in a pub with a Negro). The provision is also to be limited to coloreds. Protection of racial honor of this kind is already practiced by other *Völker*. It is well-know, for example, that the southern states of North America maintain the most stringent separation between the white population and coloreds in both public and personal interactions.[44]

There are few documents that show more provocatively how mistaken it is to imagine that American segregation law was of no interest to the Nazis. The Prussian Memorandum was the principal early statement of the radical program that eventuated in the Nuremberg Laws; there is no ignoring the fact that it made a point of citing the example of Jim Crow. Moreover, it is a striking fact

that it treated Jim Crow as *more* radical than what the Nazis themselves envisaged: The Nazi program was to be carefully restricted
to instances in which Germans and "coloreds" consorted in public;
as one radical Nazi on the drafting team declared, the proposal in
the Memorandum was in that sense "very limited";[45] by contrast,
as the Memorandum made a point of noting, Jim Crow targeted
"both public *and personal* interactions." This is the first of several
instances in which, as we shall see, the Nazis treated American race
law as too harsh to be borrowed wholesale by Nazi Germany. (Nor
was this the last mention of American law in the Memorandum; it
went on to invoke both American and Australian immigration law
in its discussion of the proposed crime of "race endangerment.")[46]

CONSERVATIVE JURISTIC RESISTANCE: GÜRTNER AND LÖSENER

The Nazi legal radicalism embodied in the Prussian Memorandum would eventually triumph at Nuremberg,[47] but at first it faced
substantial, and for a time successful, resistance from traditionally
minded lawyers. Indeed, juristic traditionalists managed to hold
the radicals at bay for some months. It may seem puzzling that any
measure of successful resistance could ever have been mounted—
had not Germany become a Nazi dictatorship?—but it is essential
to bear in mind the larger political context in the Germany of the
early 1930s. During the first months of Hitler's rule the Reich still
flew its two flags, the swastika of Nazism and the plain black, white,
and red banner symbolizing the nationalist conservatism that
was common within the powerful bureaucracy, staffed heavily by
trained lawyers. Eventually one event would make the unshackled
radicalism of the regime inescapably clear: the Night of the Long
Knives, the Nazi orgy of murders that began on June 30, 1934. After
the Night of the Long Knives it was impossible to pretend that

Germany had not cut all ties with traditional conceptions of even a minimal rule of law.[48] But before then, at least until the early summer of 1934, comparatively moderate lawyers were in a position to hold something of a line, and the record of conflict over the Prussian Memorandum shows that they did so.

In the history of lawyerly rearguard actions against Nazi radicalism, two fascinating and ambiguous figures played especially important roles: Franz Gürtner and Bernhard Lösener. These were men who made well-documented efforts to counter two critical aspects of the radical program: the criminalization of racially mixed marriages, and the expansive definition of who would count as a "Jew." Neither was a heroic figure by any means. Both were men of the far right, who collaborated with Hitler, and who were quite prepared to work toward the creation of a system of persecution of some kind. What made them relative moderates was not some commitment to liberal political values, or at least not some openly expressed commitment.[49] What the sources show instead is that they defended the traditional doctrines of the law, insisting that the Nazi program of persecution conform to the logic and strictures of the highly developed "legal science" for which Germany was famous. These were not soapbox political dissidents, but bureaucratic officeholders who displayed the instinctive conservatism of trained jurists, and who succeeded for a while in defending some of the traditional standards of German lawfulness.

To begin with Gürtner, the Minister of Justice: He was one of the nationalist conservatives who had collaborated with the Nazis and taken up posts in Nazi government. A leading member of the German National People's Party, Gürtner had been Justice Minister of Bavaria, home state of the Nazis, in the 1920s, where he had shown sympathy with Hitler, and perhaps aided him, while never joining the Nazi Party.[50] He was appointed Reich Minister of Justice by nationalist conservative Franz von Papen in the summer of 1932, and was subsequently retained first by Schleicher, and then by Hitler. He would be kept in his office until his death in 1941, joining the party only in 1937, a late representative of Nazi collaboration with nationalist conservatives. Scholars portray him as a man who remained in office out of a sincere, if hopeless, desire to obstruct the worst evils of Nazism to the extent possible.[51]

Of course it *was* hopeless; in the end Gürtner did stay in office under Hitler, and he can hardly be called a hero. Nevertheless we know that he made efforts to check Nazi radicalism in the early 1930s,[52] and in particular that he played a major role, alongside other lawyers, in raising doubts about the demand of the Prussian Memorandum that racially mixed marriages be criminalized.

It is important to describe those doubts carefully. From the point of view of conventionally trained German jurists, even ones who were perfectly willing to accept the authority of the new regime, there were far-reaching questions about whether the measures called for by the Prussian Memorandum were workable within the established norms of German law. A large part of the difficulty had to do with the sweeping magnitude of its proposals. The Prussian Memorandum demanded, in a few fiery paragraphs, that racially mixed marriages be criminalized. But how was such a criminalization possible unless racially mixed marriages were also declared civilly invalid? How could one part of the law criminalize an institution that another part treated as lawful? Rewriting the Criminal Code would entail rewriting the Civil Code as well—a daunting proposition for the conventional German jurists.[53] Moreover, declaring mixed marriages civilly invalid was no simple matter. Even the Prussian Memorandum did not suggest that the state should dissolve existing interracial marriages. Putting its proposals into effect thus meant creating a peculiar state of affairs in which some interracial marriages would remain perfectly legal while others were subject to harsh criminal punishment. That could be made to work only by means of some complex and contentious juristic gyrations.[54]

Nor did the difficulties end there. It was standard legal doctrine in Germany, as in all parts of the Western world outside the United States, that marriage was in any case ordinarily not a matter for criminal law. Bigamy had historically been prosecuted as a crime, but bigamy did not offer a model easily applicable to racially mixed marriage.[55] Indeed, for conventional lawyers like Gürtner, the contrast between bigamy and ordinary miscegenation was sharp. The crime of bigamy was close in spirit to fraud: a bigamy prosecution commonly deemed one party an innocent victim.[56] Bigamies generally took place when one spouse lied to the other about his or her marital status. There was certainly some room to generalize from the example of bigamy in the making of new Nazi law: the Prussian Memorandum suggested that the law on "race treason" should take a particular harsh line on "malicious deception," cases in which one spouse or sexual partner deceived the other about his or her race. A person who lied about his or her race was akin to a person who lied about his or her marital status. (It was also possible to cite the precedent of a 1927 law, which imposed criminal penalties on those who failed to disclose that they had a venereal disease; not revealing that you were a Jew, radical Nazis suggested, was like not revealing that you had a sexually transmitted disease.)[57] But in ordinary cases of miscegenation both parties would go into the union with open eyes, with neither having lied. How could that be criminalized? All that Minister Gürtner was willing to endorse was the criminalization of "malicious deception"—though even there conventional jurists saw serious logical difficulties.[58]

As for Bernhard Lösener: He played his part primarily with regard to the problem of defining "Jews." When it came to the classification of "mongrels," party radicals inevitably favored the most expansive definition possible, and in the July 1933 Law on the Re-

Figure 7. Bernhard Lösener. *Source*: Ullstein Bild © Getty Images.

vocation of Naturalization and the Withdrawal of German Citizenship they succeeded in declaring any person with one Jewish grandparent a "Jew."[59] This was, by the standards of Nazi policy, a far-reaching definition—though to be sure nowhere near as far-reaching as the "one-drop" rule and other racial definitions that prevailed in the American states.[60] Certainly it was too radical for moderate lawyers in the regime, who wished to take a more sparing and merciful attitude, and who pushed for less aggressive definitions over the following two years.

Lösener was first among them. Lösener was a centrally important actor in the making of the Nuremberg Laws. He served as

Judenreferent, "reporter on the Jews" for the Ministry of the Interior, and was one of the chief draftsmen of the Nuremberg Laws, and the author of an important account of the drafting process. He has been the target of considerable, and withering, criticism, since it is clear that his account of events was self-serving. Nevertheless even Lösener's harshest critics call him, jarring though the phrase may sound, an authentically "moderate" Nazi anti-Semite:[61] he would eventually resign from the office of Jewish affairs in the 1940s, be arrested in 1944 after sheltering some of the plotters against Hitler, and be expelled from the Nazi Party in 1945.[62]

This was another striking figure: the draftsman of the Nuremberg Laws who was eventually arrested and expelled from the party. Like others among his colleagues, the Lösener of the 1930s displayed conservative lawyerly instincts. Nazi though he was—and let it be emphasized that he was a reprehensible anti-Semite, an early member of the party who later tried to whitewash his record— Lösener was also a cautious and methodical jurist, and his role in the drafting process too shows how juristic conservatism could work as a brake on Nazi radicalism. During the early 1930s Lösener and other jurists fought to limit the definition of "Jew," shielding where possible persons of only half Jewish descent.[63] Those efforts, which historians have traced in engrossing detail in the archives, were only partly successful: the ultimate implementation ordinance of the Reich Citizenship Law did include some, but not all, half Jews within the disfavored status. That ordinance, completed in November 1935, distinguished between two classes: those who "were" Jews, having at least three Jewish grandparents, and those who "counted" as Jews, having two Jewish grandparents while also practicing the Jewish religion, or having chosen to marry a Jewish spouse.[64] The great bureaucratic battle over the "mongrels" thus ended in a tense compromise—but one in which even as late as

November 1935 the weight of juristic opinion represented by figures like Lösener could still make itself felt.

✹

Such was the context of the making of the Nuremberg Laws: With mob violence periodically erupting in the streets, Nazi legal officials were under pressure to draft "unambiguous" laws banning mixed marriages and sexual liaisons. Nazi leaders with an eye on foreign relations were hesitant to see the passage of provocative race legislation. Party radicals wished to criminalize all sexual mixing; moderate jurists were full of doubts. The radicals wanted an expansive definition of "Jews"; moderates resisted. In the ensuing debates, Germans went looking for foreign models, and they found the anti-miscegenation laws of the American states.

THE MEETING OF JUNE 5, 1934

Like American immigration and citizenship law, American anti-miscegenation law was very old, dating back to a pioneering Virginia statute of 1691.[65] The American tradition of banning race miscegenation, like American immigration and second-citizenship law, was attracting European attention well before the Nazis came on the scene.[66] This was another area in which America was a recognized global leader, with prohibitions both old and new. American states continued to introduce anti-miscegenation statutes in the early twentieth century; this was an active area of American racist lawmaking.[67]

And as with immigration and citizenship law, German lawyers and policy makers had a history of great interest in American anti-miscegenation law that long predated the Nazi period. The first flurry of German studies of the American approach dated to the era of pre–World War I German imperialism. Beginning in 1905, German colonial administrators in South-West Africa and elsewhere instituted anti-miscegenation measures, intended to safeguard the "purity" of the German settler population against mixing with the natives. These racist measures were unparalleled among other European colonial powers, but they had a model in America, and German colonial administrators investigated that model eagerly, as Guettel has shown in important work. Their efforts included voyages through the southern states, commissioned reports from diplomats, consultation with the Harvard historian Archibald Cary Coolidge, and more; and the colonial archives include detailed reports on US law.[68] Here once again, late nineteenth- and early twentieth-century America struck Germans as a country at the forefront of the creation of "a conscious unity of the white race."[69]

German interest in American anti-miscegenation law did not fade in the 1930s. The anti-miscegenation measures that prewar colonial administrators produced may or may not have directly influenced the Nuremberg Laws; historians disagree.[70] But there can be no doubt that the drafters of the Nuremberg Laws studied American law just as eagerly as their colonial predecessors did. America was the great model in 1905, and it remained the great model three decades later.

It is now time to turn to the details of the stenographic report of the June 5, 1934, meeting of the Commission on Criminal Law Reform.[71] This report, preserved in the archives in two separate versions, was first published in 1989.[72] The meeting it transcribed brought together seventeen lawyers and officials under the chairmanship of Justice Minister Gürtner. The attendees included Lösener, the "reporter on the Jews;" Freisler, the future President of the Nazi People's Court, at the time a State Secretary attached to the Ministry of Justice; along with other lawyers and medical doctors from the

Nazi ministries, including three radicals who had participated with Freisler in the drafting of the Prussian Memorandum.[73] The meeting was called to respond to the demands that the Memorandum had made, and the principal legal questions on the table were whether mixed marriages should be criminalized, what form any such criminalization should take, and how to manage the challenging business of defining "Jews" and other members of disfavored races, along with a few other matters that I will leave to the side.

The transcript is a record of clashes—though generally studiously polite ones—between the radicals who had worked on the Memorandum, and juristic moderates led by Justice Minister Gürtner. At the time that the meeting occurred, the Night of the Long Knives had not yet taken place. The meeting thus dates to the last weeks before the mask had fully fallen from the face of radicalism in Nazi Germany, and the transcript records a last moment of moderate success.[74] Gürtner and the other moderate lawyers present did not quarrel with the goal of institutionalizing anti-Jewish policies; these were, to say it once again, no heroes of resistance to Hitler; but they did work to fend off extremes of criminalization. Some of them suggested that perhaps a campaign of public "education and enlightenment" might gradually succeed in ending the evil of sexual mixing without formal criminalization. If there was to be criminalization at all, Gürtner insisted, it must be done on the basis of the only suitable juristic model, the criminalization of bigamy:[75] that meant that there were only to be prosecutions in cases where a Jew had engaged in "malicious deception" of an "Aryan" partner.[76] Other lawyers present pushed an even milder line: Eduard Kohlrausch, a prominent professor of criminal law, argued that criminalization of any kind would be actively counterproductive.[77] Lösener maintained, in line with traditional juristic teachings, that the very concept of a "Jew" was so elusive that the radical program was impracticable.[78]

For their part, the radicals present argued, occasionally in brow-beating tones, that the Criminal Code must be revised to reflect the "fundamental principle of National Socialism," that was the harsh legal enforcement of racism;[79] but at the end of the day they were forced to give up on the full-scale implementation of the Prussian Memorandum. Some of them admitted that diplomatic pressures made it impossible, for the moment, to carry out the measures that they deemed necessary; the objections of so many countries to targeting "colored Races" were too grave.[80] Freisler, while insisting fervently on the need to remain faithful to the mission of national socialism and defending the use of the term "colored," yielded to the technical objections of the conventional jurists: for the moment there could only be the creation of the offense of "malicious deception."[81] At the same time that the radicals were making these concessions, though, they were also making unmistakably threatening noises. There were menacing references to the political agitation taking place outside the meeting.[82] Freisler hinted, courteously but ominously, that the ultimate judgment would have to be made not by the professional jurists present, but by the "political decision" of the Nazi leadership.[83] If the moderate lawyers were able to hold the line at this meeting, it is clear enough in retrospect that the political forces were arrayed against them.

And what about the place of American law, already cited by the Prussian Memorandum? The dismaying answer is that this pivotal meeting on the road to the Nuremberg Laws involved repeated and detailed discussion of the American example, from its very opening moments, and that American law was championed principally by the radicals.

After a brief opening statement by Gürtner, the meeting heard from two officials who had been charged with preparing reports for the commission. The first was Fritz Grau, a party member, later to rise to high rank in the SS.[84] Grau, one of the men who had participated in the drafting of the Prussian Memorandum, took a hardline view of the need for criminalization. But, like other hardliners present, he conceded that it was not yet possible to implement the program of the Prussian Memorandum. "Painful" though it was for him to say so, he declared, for the moment foreign relations made it necessary to hold off on including "race protection" explicitly in the Criminal Code.[85]

But that did not mean that Grau was ready to abandon the field to the forces of moderation; he was still determined to lay out the unsparing Nazi case against the Jewish menace. Grau acknowledged there were some lawyers and officials who believed that a program of "education and enlightenment" would suffice as an alternative to criminalization. "Education and enlightenment" was, however, he said, an unacceptable approach. Like other Nazis, Grau linked the question of sexual mixing to the question of citizenship, just as the two would be linked at Nuremberg. Here is the record of his words:

The Party Program [of 1920] determines that citizens may only be persons of German descent, and that foreign races should be subject to a guest right. The Program thus intends that the new German state should be built on a racial foundation. In order to achieve this goal, a great deal has taken place over the last years. An effort has been made to root out the racially foreign elements from the body of the *Volk*, first of all by striving to deprive them of any influence, to drive them out of the leadership of the state as well as out of other influential positions and professions. . . .

All these measures have undoubtedly brought us a step forward; but they have not achieved and could not achieve an effective quarantine separating the racially foreign elements in Germany from the people of German descent. For foreign policy reasons the necessary law could not be instituted—a law that would prevent all sexual mixing between Germans and the foreign races.

Now one could perhaps say—and here I come to the second question posed by Mr. Minister of Justice—that this goal could be achieved gradually through education and enlightenment without any express law.[86]

It was at this point that Grau turned to America, the homeland of race-based law. He noted that Jim Crow segregation, already put on the table by the Prussian Memorandum, might seem to offer a possible model for an approach founded on "education and enlightenment." However, it was his view that segregation was not suitable to German circumstances:

Other *Völker* too, one might say, had achieved such a goal [i.e., of the elimination of race mixing through education and enlightenment] essentially through social segregation. That statement is however only correct with certain provisos. Among these other *Völker*—I am thinking chiefly of North America, which even has statutes along these lines—the problem is a different one, namely the problem of keeping members of colored races at bay, a problem that plays as good as no role for us in Germany. For us the problem is sharply directed against the Jews, who must be kept enduringly apart, since there is no doubt that they represent a foreign body in the *Volk*. It is my conviction that just taking the path of social segregation and separation will never achieve the goal, as long as the Jews in Germany represent a thoroughly extraordinary economic power. As long as they have a voice in economic affairs in our German Fatherland, as they do now, as long as they have the most beautiful automobiles, the most beautiful motorboats, as long as they play a prominent role in all pleasure spots and resorts, and everywhere that costs money, as long as all this is true I do not believe that they can really be segregated from the body of the German *Volk* in the absence of statutory law. This can only be achieved through positive statutory measures that forbid absolutely all sexual mixing of a Jew with a German, and impose severe criminal punishment.[87]

Thus, riveting to read, a hardline Nazi view on Jim Crow segregation: Segregation would simply never succeed in Germany. German Jews, unlike American blacks, were too wealthy and arrogant; the only hope was that they be put down by "severe criminal punishment." Jim Crow segregation—such was this striking Nazi judgment—was a strategy that could work only against a minority population that was already oppressed and impoverished.

It deserves emphasis that Grau went out of his way to dismiss the option of Jim Crow segregation: The fact that he felt obliged to do so suggests clearly enough that there had been debates about American law behind the scenes before this meeting took place. Somebody had been making the case for a German Jim Crow as the foundation of comparatively mild approach aiming at "education and enlightenment" of the population. Indeed we shall see momentarily that Grau was not the only participant at the meeting to address the possible attractions of Jim Crow.[88] When Grau had finished his report, Kohlrausch then followed with his own distinctly more moderate one, which pled the case against criminalization.[89]

Minister of Justice Gürtner then took the floor to open the general discussion. His intervention revealed that the ministry had been working hard to collect information on the very American example that Grau had brought up:

I am very grateful to the two gentlemen for their reports.... If I were to express a few thoughts myself, they would be these.

When it comes to race legislation it was naturally very attractive to look around in the world to see how this problem has been attacked by other *Völker*.

I possess here a thoroughly comprehensible synoptic presentation of North American race legislation, and I can tell you right away that the material was rather difficult to find. If any of you gentlemen takes a personal interest, I am ready to make this breakdown available to you.[90]

Apparently Gürtner displayed a Justice Ministry memo surveying the law of the American states. Then as now, collecting information on all of the states was "rather difficult." Nevertheless the ministry had been able to extract what German lawyers always seek, a "Grundgedanke," a "fundamental idea":

The material gives an answer to the question of what form race legislation in the American states takes. The picture is as variegated as the American map. Almost all American states have race legislation. The races that must be defended against are characterized in different ways. Nevertheless a fundamental idea can be very easily extracted. The laws list Negroes or mulattoes or Chinese or Mongols in motley variation. They often speak of persons of African descent, thus addressing the issue historically, by which they mean Negroes, and there are a few sections which make positive reference to the Caucasian race. That is not uninteresting; since I believe there is a jurisprudence on the question of whether Jews belong to the Caucasian race.[91]

At that point, Gürtner apparently turned to his deputy Hans von Dohnanyi, perhaps the most fascinating, and certainly the most heroic, of the moderates present. Dohnanyi, the son of the Hungarian composer Ernő Dohnanyi and brother-in-law of the dissident theologian Dietrich Bonhoeffer, joined the Nazi Justice Ministry in June 1933. But only a few weeks after the June 5, 1934, meeting, he became a clandestine opponent of the regime, embarking on the dangerous project of collecting and indexing documents that he hoped would someday be used for a prosecution of the Nazi leadership.[92] Eventually he would be executed for participation in the resistance against Hitler.[93]

In early June 1934, however, Dohnanyi was still a government legal official at work on the creation of anti-Jewish legislation. Evidently he had had some of the responsibility for the ministry's research, for he supplied an account of American race jurisprudence as to Jews:

> State Attorney Dr. von Dohnanyi: Yes, the jurisprudence speaks of the Caucasian race simply in opposition to all colored races, that is to say it speaks of the white race, and since Jews belong to the white race they are reckoned among the Caucasians.
> Reich Minister of Justice Gürtner: That is the jurisprudence of the highest courts?
> State Attorney Dr. Dohnanyi: Yes.
> [Gürtner]: One can see from that, and from the map, how correct the observation of Mr. Vice President Dr. Grau was, that this legislation is not directed against Jews, but protects the Jews. That gives us nothing to work with; the aim [of an American-style approach] would be the contrary [of our own].[94]

If that were all that the participants had had to say about American law, we would have to conclude that the American model, carefully researched by the Justice Ministry, had proven of no value to the Nazi regime. But Gürtner did not stop with the observation that American legislation was not directed against the Jews, and he would not be the last to raise the subject. He continued with his presentation of the ministry memo, turning to what was "interesting" about American law. The ministry's research had turned up many facts about American anti-miscegenation statutes: "Then it is interesting," Gürtner reported, "to see what legal consequences are attached to sexual union. That too is variable. All sorts of expressions appear: 'illegal' and 'void,' 'absolutely void,' 'utterly null and void.' 'Prohibited' also sometimes appears. From these shifting and not very sharply juristically defined words it can be seen that civil law consequences attach in all cases, and criminal consequences in a great number of cases."[95] This was the critical point: In America there were "criminal consequences." The American example spoke directly to the great question that divided the lawyers present at the meeting. It showed that the criminalization of racially mixed marriages, even outside the case of bigamy, was not unprecedented. That fact cannot have been welcome to Gürtner, who opposed such far-reaching criminalization, and he quickly made an effort to neutralize the American example. Whatever American statutes might say, Gürtner rushed to argue, it could not really be the case that Americans routinely imposed such "criminal consequences" in practice: "A question that cannot be answered on the basis of our research is how criminal law race protections are applied in practice. It seems to me that the snapshot we have here does not in practice always correspond to the reality."[96] Gürtner simply refused to concede that the Americans actually went so far as to prosecute miscegenists. He had no evidence for that assertion,[97] but we should understand that he was doing his best to grasp at some argument that would deflect the impact of the American precedent.

Gürtner then returned to the question of anti-Jewish legislation. The United States, he reported, was not alone in refusing to engage in formal legal persecution of Jews: "We have not been able to find race legislation aimed at combatting the Jews in any currently existing foreign law, among the states which were the object of our research. I believe that in order to find such legislation, we would have to go back to the law of the medieval German cities."[98] It was true enough that there was no anti-Jewish legislation in the United States; but then, there was no anti-Jewish legislation in any contemporary system. What was nevertheless "interesting," much though Gürtner wished to minimize it, was that America had produced the very sort of law that Nazi lawyers had gathered at the meeting to debate: it had taken the step of criminalizing race mixing "in a great number of cases."

After Gürtner's presentation of the ministry's memo, the participants moved on to a variety of technical questions in the drafting of criminal measures; it is certainly not the case that America was the sole subject of discussion, even if it was the first. Nevertheless, it was not forgotten. References to American law continued to pepper the meeting.[99] Most especially, the transcript reveals that as the morning wore on, the American example was highlighted by two of the more aggressively racist Nazis at the meeting, Freisler and Karl Klee, Presiding Criminal Court Judge and Professor of Criminal Law at the University of Berlin, and another of the radicals who had worked on the Prussian Memorandum.[100] It seems that the United States had particular attractions for the more uncompromising racists present.

Thus about two-thirds of the way through the meeting Klee turned once again to Jim Crow segregation and its value for Germany. The question that concerned Klee was whether the new Nazi criminal law regime should be race-*based*, simply declaring the separation of the races, or rac*ist*, declaring the superiority of some races and the inferiority of others. Some Nazis had suggested that the new law should be purely race-based: avoiding any claim that Jews were inferior, they argued, would improve Germany's international public relations.[101] Klee rejected that approach. The plain truth, he insisted, was that the German people were convinced that the Jews were an inferior race, and German law should say so openly. Here, Klee believed that America offered a valuable model. American race law, he argued, was unquestionably founded on a belief in racial inferiority: like the Supreme Court in *Brown v. Board of Education*, Klee had no doubt that Jim Crow was designed to dramatize the inferiority of the black population.[102] Klee viewed segregation as a form of Nazi-style "race protection," intended to alert the white population to the menace posed by blacks. Jim Crow, he argued, was the American equivalent of one of the principal "race protection" strategies Nazis were using on the German streets in 1933–34, the boycott. Nazi storm troopers aimed to "educate and enlighten" the populace by staging intimidating boycotts in front of Jewish shops.[103] Under Jim Crow, Klee argued, Americans were doing the same thing, but on a grander social scale: "American race legislation too [just like German popular attitudes] certainly does not base itself on the idea of [mere] racial difference, but, to the extent this legislation is aimed against Negroes and others, absolutely certainly on the idea of the inferiority of the other race, in the face of which the purity of the American race must be protected. This is also expressed in the social boycott that is mounted on all sides in America against the Negroes."[104] Here was another striking Nazi interpretation: Segregation was the American version of the Nazi boycott. American racists employed Jim Crow law "on all sides" in order to raise American consciousness, just as Nazi thugs stood outside Jewish shops brandishing placards reading "Germans! Defend yourselves!

Don't buy from Jews!" It was yet another case of Americans "defending" themselves against "an alien race that [was] attempting to gain the upper hand" and threatening to exert "influence." And what the American example showed was that true race-based criminal law ought to be unapologetically racist criminal law.

But by far the most dramatic exploitation of the American example came a few minutes later, from Freisler, the judicial "murderer in the service of Hitler." His intervention suggested that he too, like Gürtner, had come to the meeting prepared to debate America, and with detailed knowledge of the American case in hand.

Freisler used the American example to mount a Nazi response to the objections of traditionally minded jurists like Lösener. It was a fundamental principle of traditional German law that criminal law required clear and unambiguous concepts: if judges were permitted to convict on the basis of vague concepts, the core requirements of the rule of law would not be met.[105] Yet—so Lösener argued at the meeting—Nazi policy makers had failed to find a clear and unambiguous concept of a "Jew." There was simply no accepted scientific means of determining who was "Jewish": "An effective means of determining whether a given human being has an element of Jewishness on the basis of his behavior or outward appearance [Habitus] or blood or the like does not exist, or at least at present has not yet been found."[106] That failure constituted an obstacle for criminalization: it was intolerable, Lösener declared, to allow every individual judge to make decisions on the basis of mere *Gefühlsantisemitismus*, of vague sentiments of Jew hatred.[107] The indispensable prerequisite for proper criminalization was a clearly delineated and scientifically acceptable definition of who counted as a racial Jew.[108] In any case judges, Lösener added, must work within the limits of the presumption of innocence.[109] These were basic requirements of legality, and they stood in the way of implementing the radical Nazi program.

It was here that Freisler, showing typically bluff radical Nazi contempt for technical doctrinal concerns, countered by citing the United States. The problem, Freisler maintained, along with another radical companion, was not a "scientific" or "theoretical" matter at all. It was a problem that called for a purely "primitive" and "political" response[110]—and American law was Freisler's model of the "primitive" and "political." American law, he said, demonstrated that it was perfectly possible to have racist legislation even if it was technically infeasible to come up with a scientifically satisfactory definition of race. Freisler went into intimate detail about the laws of the American states, and the nature of American jurisprudence, to make his point:

> Now as far as the delineation of the race concept goes, it is interesting to take a look at this list of the American states. Thirty of the states of the Union have race legislation, which, it seems clear to me, is crafted from the point of view of race protection. ["And political!" added another radical who had worked on the Prussian Memorandum.][111] That is perhaps [the case] only with regard to the Japanese, but in other respects from the racial point of view. Proof: North Carolina has also forbidden marriages between Indians and Negroes; that has after all certainly been done from the point of view of race protection. . . . I believe that apart from the desire to exclude foreign political influence that is possibly becoming too powerful, which I can imagine is the case with regard to the Japanese, this is all from the point of view of race protection. . . .[112]

This American form of "race protection," Freisler continued, did not trouble itself about the correct scientific conceptualization of race:

> Moreover it is not the case that all states that have to reckon with the possibility of Japanese immigration have spoken of

the Japanese, but some have spoken of Mongols, even though it is without a doubt the case that Japanese and Chinese are not to be assigned to the Mongols, but to an entirely different *Volk* blood group. Why have these states done this? I cannot believe that they have done it just in order to delineate a concept. Rather I believe that they have done it, because they were targeting a kind of race image [*Rassebild*], and have only erroneously lumped the Japanese in with the Mongols. The same thing is shown by the way they list them [i.e., the various races] all together. A state speaks of Mongols, Negroes or mulattoes. That clearly shows that the racial point of view has been placed in the foreground. . . . The bottom line is that the Americans in reality have first and foremost desired to have race legislation, even if today they would perhaps like to pretend it is not so.[113]

At any rate, he explained, the beauty of the American example was that it demonstrated, as American law so often does, that it was possible to manage a functioning legal system without the sorts of clear concepts German lawyers cherished:

How have they gone about doing this? They have used different means. Several states have simply employed geographical concepts. One state speaks of African descent, another of persons from Africa, Korea or Malaysia. Still others have conflated matters, combining geographical origin with their conception of a particular circle of blood relatedness. For example in the example I have just given there is subsequently added: or of Mongolian race. Another state mentions both alongside each other: Nevada speaks of Ethiopians or of the black race, Malaysians or of the brown race, Mongols or of the yellow race. That signifies a remarkable mixing of the system of geographical origins with conceptualization on the basis of blood relatedness.[114]

Yet all this conceptual messiness did not prevent America from having a racist order. American legislation, Freisler argued, managed perfectly well with what might be called the "political construction of race":[115] it displayed an ideological determination to build a racist order even in the face of the absence of any meaningful scientific conception of race, and in that regard Freisler believed that Germany had something to learn from American legislative techniques.

Nor was it just American legislation that had lessons to offer. Freisler further argued that there was something to learn from the techniques of American judging. American judges had no trouble applying racist law despite its fuzzy concepts. Indeed, if it were not for the lack of American attention to the Jewish problem, the American style of jurisprudence, Freisler declared in a resonant sentence, would "suit us perfectly":

> These states obviously all have an absolutely unambiguous jurisprudence, and this jurisprudence would suit us perfectly [*würde für uns vollkommen passen*], with a single exception. Over there they have in mind, practically speaking, only coloreds and half-coloreds, which includes mestizos and mulattoes; but the Jews, who are also of interest to us, are not reckoned among the coloreds. I have not seen that any state speaks of foreign race [as standard Nazi language would dictate] but instead they name the races in some more primitive way.[116]

The absence of an anti-Jewish jurisprudence did not mean, however, that American jurisprudence had nothing to teach Germany. What the American example showed was that German judges could persecute Jews even without legislation founded in clear and scientifically satisfactory definitions. "Primitive" concept formation would suffice. In fact, Freisler maintained, it would be perfectly workable if German race legislation too, following the American lead, simply specified "coloreds":

It seems to me doubtful that there would be any need to expressly mention the Jews alongside the coloreds. I believe that
every judge would reckon the Jews among the coloreds, even
though they look outwardly white, just as they do the Tatars,
who are not yellow. Therefore I am of the opinion that we can
proceed with the same primitivity [*Primitivität*] that is used
by these American states. A state even simply says: "colored
people." Such a procedure would be crude [*roh*], but it would
suffice.[117]

Such was the attractiveness of the American common-law model
for this baleful figure, the avatar of the modern judicial butcher, a
man guilty of "a perversion of the forms of justice that was extreme
even by the standards of the Third Reich".[118] American courts did
not allow themselves to be hobbled by some pedantic insistence
on clear and juristically or scientifically defensible concepts of race.
They just went to work. Even though America did not target the
Jews, this American common-law style of legal racism, with its
easygoing, open-ended, know-it-when-I-see-it way with the law, had
a "primitivity" that would "suit" Nazi judges "perfectly."

This was too much for Gürtner, who responded to Freisler by
trying once again to dismiss the usefulness of American "models":
"Well, the idea that we could get anything useful from these American models cannot be exploited in practice, since, as Herr State Secretary Dr. Freisler has already said, American law concerns itself with
variants, with different nuances, of the concept 'coloreds,' used now
in this way, now in that, perhaps most clearly in the case of Virginia,
which speaks of 'coloured persons,' including mulattoes, mestizos
etc."[119] Such vague reference to "coloreds" was useless to Germany,
Gürtner insisted, and it was useless because there should be no general criminalization of racially mixed marriages. The only possible
aim of the new legislation would be to criminalize malicious racial

deception in marriage, and it was in the nature of things that "coloured persons" were in no position to deceive others about their race: "If our aim in the criminal law of race protection is to punish malicious deception, then the question of coloreds falls *ipso facto* by the wayside, since malicious deception on the part of coloreds does not seem to me very probable."[120] The American question was thus sharply framed as part of the conflict between hardliner and moderate. Freisler, the champion of merciless criminalization and "primitive" rather than juristic decision making, declared that the American approach would "suit us perfectly"; Gürtner, the lawyer-moderate, still in the saddle in early June 1934, but destined to lose in the political battles of the coming year, insisted that there was no place for "American models" in the more modest and juristically conventional approach he advocated.

The meeting included further references to American law that I will not discuss in full here. Among them, though, there is one exchange, toward the end of the day, that stands out. Erich Möbius, a Nazi doctor attached to the Interior Ministry,[121] raised once again, sorrowfully, the difficulties caused by foreign objections to the criminalization of consorting with "colored races"—and reported, memorably, on a conversation with an American, to which Freisler gave his own memorable response. Möbius's American acquaintance had observed that the Nazis' diplomatic troubles were caused by the explicit racism of the Nazi program, and asked whether it was necessary to be quite so open:

> Dr. Möbius: I am reminded of something an American said to us recently. He explained, "We do the same thing you are doing. But why do you have to say it so explicitly in your laws?" State Secretary Freisler: But the Americans put it in their own laws even more explicitly![122]

Indeed.

Figure 8. A meeting of the Commission on Criminal Law Reform, 1936. Center, wearing a swastika armband, is Roland Freisler. Next to him, with cigar, is Justice Minister Franz Gürtner. *Source*: Ullstein Bild © Getty Images.

✦

Thus a stenographic transcript of a critical meeting planning what would become the Nuremberg Laws. The transcript is quite a striking datum in comparative law: it is rare indeed that we possess such an ingenuous and detailed record of how the process of influence transpires.

And needless to say what the June 5 transcript records is not evidence of the "astonishing insignificance" of American law. American law was the first topic of discussion at the meeting, and it was mooted in notably well-informed detail by the participants,

including numerous verbatim quotes from anti-miscegenation statutes from all over the United States. Moreover the American example, already highlighted by the Prussian Memorandum in September 1933, had clearly been a subject of discussion and debate
before the meeting took place, so much so that the Justice Ministry
had gone out of its way to prepare a detailed memo on the subject.
In particular it is clear that there had been debates over whether
the importation of Jim Crow measures might not serve to "educate
and enlighten" the German populace. Some moderates had advocated Jim Crow "enlightenment" as an alternative to criminalization, while a hardline figure like Klee thought of Jim Crow as a
more broad-gauged version of the menacing Nazi boycott. Justice
Minister Gürtner was manifestly uncomfortable with "American
models," but he cited them nevertheless, sometimes in significant
detail, just as Freisler did.[123] Moreover Gürtner felt constrained to
open the general discussion at the meeting by presenting the ministry's memo. In particular he felt constrained to note that the
American states engaged in the otherwise rare practice of the criminalization of racially mixed marriages. The meeting was certainly
not by any means devoted exclusively to America; but the participants clearly took a serious interest in what they could learn from
the laws of the American states, and discussed them repeatedly, and
it is unmistakably the case that the American example was pushed
hardest by the radical faction, which lost out for the moment, but
which would ultimately triumph at Nuremberg fifteen months
later.

The transcript, be it said, does not record an effort at generat-
ing international propaganda by citing the American example. The
participants unquestionably were worried about "foreign policy"
considerations; but they were a drafting commission for criminal
law, and the purpose of their closed-door meeting, and in particular of their effort to undertake the "rather difficult" business of col-

lecting American law, was to find "material" for the making of their own Nazi legislation.

All this certainly does not mean that the Blood Law was mechanically copied from the law of some American state, but it can hardly be written off. What it suggests, clearly enough, is that for radical Nazi lawyers in the summer of 1934, as for Hitler in the 1920s, America was the obvious preeminent example of a "race state," even if it was one whose lessons were not unproblematically applicable to Germany. The bottom line is this: when the leading Nazi jurists assembled in early June 1934 to debate how to institutionalize racism in the new Third Reich, they began by asking how the Americans did it.

THE SOURCES OF NAZI KNOWLEDGE OF AMERICAN LAW

A tantalizing question about the meeting remains. Where did the participants get their information? What has become of the "thoroughly comprehensible synoptic presentation of American race legislation" that Gürtner presented at the meeting? What was the source of the "list" of the laws of the thirty states that Freisler mentioned? The originals of the document or documents in question have doubtless perished, but they can be reconstructed with fair confidence, and they tell us some interesting things about the diffusion of American racist ideas in the mid-twentieth century.

It seems likely that Gürtner and Freisler were relying in part on a table listing the law of the American states that was published a few months later in the *National Socialist Handbook on Law and Legislation*, to which I will return shortly.[124] As for the ministry's memo: it is clear that it drew on the research of a man I have already mentioned several times, Heinrich Krieger, to whom a reference was later added in a redacted version of the stenographic transcript,[125] and it is important to turn for a moment to Krieger's biography, for knowing Nazi engagement with American law in the early 1930s means knowing Heinrich Krieger.

Krieger was a young Nazi lawyer who had just returned to Germany from Arkansas, where he spent two semesters as an exchange student at the University of Arkansas Law School in 1933–34.[126] He was deeply immersed in American law, so much so that in 1935 he published a well-wrought English-language article in the *George Washington Law Review* titled "Principles of the Indian Law."[127] When he returned home to the Germany in the throes of the "National Revolution," he benefited from the sponsorship of Otto Koellreutter, among others, and became a fellow at an academic institute in Düsseldorf under the control of Frick's Ministry of the Interior.[128] It was during his time in Düsseldorf that Krieger's work came to the attention of Gürtner's Ministry of Justice. He published his magnum opus on American law, *Race Law in the United States*, in 1936, and then left Germany once again to continue his research on foreign race regimes. Joining the National Socialist Office of Race Policy, he traveled to South-West Africa, where German colonial administrators had first investigated the American race law model thirty years earlier.[129] Krieger spent two productive years in Africa, publishing studies on local race law and the treatment of indigenous legal traditions, while collecting research for an extensive monograph on South Africa, a "Nordic" state, as he wrote, that was on the road to becoming a great power.[130] He returned to Germany in 1939, just in time for the outbreak of hostilities, and served with the forces of his country in a war that he described as perhaps "the most important turning point in the entire evolution" of the race question.[131] After the war was lost, Krieger's life took a new direction. In the 1950s we discover him as a prominent schoolteacher, with a changed profile: he has become a vocal proponent of international understanding and peace, advocating for European unification, while organizing student exchanges and aid for developing countries in Africa and Asia.[132] What the internationalist Krieger of the 1950s had to say about his younger Nazi self we do not know.

The writings of his youth showed a deep allegiance to Nazi values. They also showed Krieger's command of the finest techniques of advanced German scholarship. Nazi law was marked by a strong commitment to what Americans call "Legal Realism," the style of legal scholarship that also dominated in New Deal America. (I will return to the comparison between these two legal realisms in the Conclusion.) Legal Realism in the 1930s was an approach that looked beyond the black letter of the law in the effort to grapple with larger social and cultural forces. The young Krieger was a prime representative of the Nazi strain of realism. Indeed his interpretation of America is one of the more impressive examples of Nazi writing in the realist vein.

Krieger's work interpreting American law begins with his *George Washington Law Review* article on Indian law. This was a legal realist study whose aim was to identify the underlying social values that could explain what otherwise would seem incoherent black letter doctrine. The young Nazi lawyer, profiting from his year of research in the law library at the University of Arkansas in Fayetteville, presented a careful and learned review of the history of American Indian law, whose point was to expose the ultimate incoherence of the formal law. There was only one way to make sense of the jarring contradictions in American Indian law, Krieger argued: it simply had to be understood as a species of race law, founded in the unacknowledged conviction that Indians were racially different and therefore necessarily subject to a distinct legal regime.[133] The article makes for sinister reading, in light of Nazi history: setting up a distinct legal/racial regime for the Jews was of course the core idea of the Nuremberg laws, and the American treatment of the Indians was later to be invoked as a precedent for German conquests in the East. What horror we all ought to feel when we learn that Hans Frank referred to the Jews of Ukraine as "Indians" in 1942.[134] But while Krieger's interpretation may have been sinister, it was not stupid: there is nothing foolish about detecting racism at work in American Indian law.

His *Race Law in the United States* was another work that cannot be called stupid. That book, filled though it was with ugly Nazi judgments, was a work of real learning and numerous insights. Heinrich Krieger was, as it were, the Nazi Gunnar Myrdal; and his book would deserve at least a partial translation today. In it, he provided an account of American legal history presented against a richly described socioeconomic background. The book makes for startling reading today—startling, if for no other reason, because Krieger's heroes were Thomas Jefferson and Abraham Lincoln. *Race Law in the United States* was the legal companion to the Nazi world histories that credited the Founding with the creation of "the strongest prop for the Aryan struggle for world domination"; it was a heroic interpretation of American history as a long, though deeply troubled, struggle against race mixing, led by America's greatest presidents.

Jefferson was already featuring in Krieger's work in 1934, which highlighted his 1821 declaration of the impossibility of racial coexistence: "[i]t is certain that the two races, equally free, cannot live in the same government."[135] *Race Law in the United States* added an account of the Civil War era that included an exact and lengthy documentation of Lincoln's pre-1863 declarations to the effect that the only real hope for America was the resettlement of the black population elsewhere.[136] This was telling material in the Germany of the Nuremberg Laws: the Nazi policy with regard to the German Jews was precisely that they must be driven out of the Reich. Lincoln was Krieger's exemplary statesman, to whom he referred reverently: he maintained that America could have become a truly healthy race-based order if only Lincoln, wise in the knowledge that the races could not inhabit the same country, had not been assassinated.[137] Krieger's villains were the Radical Republicans, and his ultimate diagnosis of America in the 1930s was another piece of Nazi legal realism. The Radical Republicans had saddled America with the highly formalistic jurisprudence of the Fourteenth Amendment, founded on an abstract concept of equality foreign to human experience, and certainly foreign to the basic racist worldview of the American populace. The result was that American law was torn between two "shaping forces": formalistic liberal egalitarianism and realistic racism.[138] It was to be hoped that realistic racism would ultimately win out.

This was certainly a deeply distasteful reading of American legal history, but there were plenty of Americans who believed something like it at the time, both in the North and in the South.[139] Krieger's book was moreover buttressed by three hundred fifty pages of detailed study of American statutory and decisional law, accompanied by statistical and qualitative studies in American society, and it was rich in theoretical sophistication and acute observations about workings of American legal racism. It may sound grating to speak of "first-rate Nazi scholarship," but that is what Heinrich Krieger's *Race Law in the United States* represented. Krieger was only one of many fine legal scholars whose gifts did not immunize them to the draw of Nazism.

The transcript of the June 1934 planning meeting shows the stamp of young Krieger's influence. The "material" that Gürtner quoted most likely came from research included in another Krieger article, also titled "Race Law in the United States," published in mid-1934 in a technical journal of administrative law, the *Verwaltungsarchiv*, and thereafter regularly cited by Nazi policy makers.[140] That article is a compendium of what was known in Germany in the summer of 1934. Krieger reviewed for his readers the harsh tenor of American anti-miscegenation law in the early 1930s:

> The attempt to enter into an unlawful mixed marriage has the almost universal legal consequence of both invalidity and exposure to criminal punishment. With regard to the first of these consequences the statutes use the following terms, either individually or in combination: void, unlawful, null, illegal, absolutely void. The reach of the civil invalidity is not defined in a uniform way, but illegitimacy and incapacity to inherit of the offspring are the regular results.
>
> Violations of these marriage prohibitions are threatened with both fines and imprisonment. Statutes that provide for both forms of punishment sometimes permit both to be imposed, sometimes threaten them in the alternative. There is a corresponding variation in the grading of the offense, for example misdemeanor in Nevada, felony in Tennessee, felony (infamous crime) in Maryland, and in the measure of punishment. In several states imprisonment of up to ten years may be imposed, in others six months is the highest possible sentence. In a few states (Missouri, Indiana) the law expressly uses the concept of knowing violation of the law, a provision that rests on the recognition that there is widespread ignorance of the descent of individuals.[141]

It was presumably this passage, or some version of it, that Gürtner had before him at the June 5 meeting.

Krieger's article also made a point of emphasizing the open-ended and "not very sharply juristically defined" approach of American law, dwelling on the fact that American law was content to divide the population into two fundamentally arbitrary categories, "white" and "colored." Like Freisler, Krieger emphasized that there was nothing scientific about these concepts: the two categories were the product of "artificial line-drawing," not race reality. Nevertheless American law was able to manage as it wrestled with the same critical "problem" as Germany: how to treat "mongrels": "The problem of the legal treatment of *mongrels* has received a simple solution, at least from the point of view of American statutory law: A fundamental distinction is made between only *two* population groups: *whites* and *coloreds*. All of the concepts used in the regulations accordingly involve artificial line-drawing, partly by statute, partly by the courts." Implicit in this was the point made by Dohnanyi at the June 5 meeting: the fact that there were only two categories meant that American law lumped Jews in under the heading "Caucasian." As Krieger would explain in *Race Law in the United States*, this was because the United States had "so far" not gotten around to the Jew problem.[142] In his 1934 article, however, Krieger did not pause over the question of the Jews. Like Gürtner and Freisler he simply moved on to what was "interesting" in the many techniques that the American states used for addressing the definitional challenges posed by their "enormous mass of mongrels." For the most part, Krieger reported, the states looked to descent, defined by fractions of blood, but they sometimes took other tacks as well:

> States that draw racial distinctions determine membership in the colored group either according to degrees of descent from a colored ascendant or according to the percentage of colored blood. In line with this the laws of four states define coloreds as "persons who descend from a Negro for up to three generations, even though one ancestor in each generation is white." Five states make a simpler determination: "Coloreds are persons who have 1/8 or more Negro blood." In two states we find the proportion to be 1/4. Occasionally the smallest admixture of "African blood" suffices to give rise to the legal classification

as colored. Other states permit outward characteristics to be decisive in determining membership in this or that population group, e.g., former slave status (North Carolina), the fact of regular social association with one or another group (ditto) or, in the case of a second marriage, the racial identity of the first marital partner (Texas).

Again like Freisler, Krieger emphasized the open-endedness of American case law:

> The conceptualization of race in the *courts* is even more variable. A rare example of an extreme case of a judicial definition is a decision from Ohio which declares white persons to include those of more than half white descent.[143] There is a growing tendency in judicial practice to assign a person to the group of coloreds whenever there is even a trace of visible Negro physical features, and beyond that to do so when the Negro descent of the individual is common knowledge, without regard to how far the degree of descent reaches back.[144]

Here again the memo that Gürtner brought to the June 5 meeting presumably included this passage or something like it.

It is true enough that Krieger's 1934 account was not about Jews as such; indeed it did not even mention them. But you would have to be willfully obtuse to deny that it was meant to inform Nazi policy discussions. It is particularly noteworthy that Krieger's article provided meat for the discussion of the "variable" "conceptualization of race" in American law of the kind that Freisler praised. In this regard his article was typical: as we shall see in a moment, there were plenty of Nazi observers who thought there was something to learn from the American approach to "mongrels," even if the Americans had "so far" not understood the imperative of putting down their Jews.

Nazi engagement with the American model continued over the subsequent months leading up to the formal proclamation of the Nuremberg Laws in September 1935. Almost as striking as the discussion of American law by the Commission on Criminal Law Reform in the summer of 1934 is Herbert Kier's article on "*Volk*, Race and State," in the *National Socialist Handbook for Law and Legislation*, whose treatment of American immigration law was already quoted in Chapter 1. More quotes are in order here. Kier began by alluding to the foreign incomprehension of Nazi goals:

> The national socialist ideology presented here, and the conclusions that must be drawn from it, have been widely met with complete misunderstanding, and National Socialism and the German *Volk* have been the targets of serious attacks. This is all the more incomprehensible since the United States of North America in particular has introduced statutory regulation in many areas that grow out of the racial point of view. In this regard it is worth observing that the dominant political ideology in the USA must be characterized as entirely liberal and democratic. With an ideology of that kind, which starts from the fundamental proposition of the equality of everything that bears a human countenance, it is all the more astonishing how extensive race legislation is in the USA. Let me provide a few examples. The laws of the following American states forbid mixed marriages between white and colored races.[145]

Kier then printed a two-page alphabetical table with exact description and citation of the anti-miscegenation legislation of all thirty American states.[146] That table corresponds to the description of American law given by Gürtner and Freisler the previous June, and it seems a fair guess that it was one of the sources of their detailed information on American law, very likely the "list" to which Freisler referred at the June 5 meeting. The same table would continue to circulate in later years, reappearing in a standard commentary on the Blood Law.[147] After printing it, Kier continued,

> Thus the 30 states listed here all have prohibitions on miscegenation, which with a single exception all pursue the aim of safeguarding the American population of European origin against race-mixing with non-European races. Only in North Carolina is there in addition a prohibition on miscegenation between Indians and Negroes. Extramarital sex between members of different races is also forbidden in several states, or even subjected to criminal punishment, for example in Alabama and Arkansas.[148]

Here we have it again: detailed Nazi engagement with the specifics of American law. Kier's next topic was segregation. He expressed some astonishment at the lengths to which American segregation was sometimes taken:

> In most of the Southern states of the Union white children and colored children are sent to different schools following statutory regulations. Most American states further demand that race be given in birth certificates, marriage licenses, and death certificates. Many American states even go so far as to require by statute segregated facilities for coloreds and whites in waiting rooms, train cars, sleeping cars, street cars, buses, steamboats, and even in prisons and jails. In several states, as in Florida, only whites can be members of militia, in yet others, as in Arkansas, voter lists are separated by race and in the same state whites and coloreds are separated on the tax rolls.[149]

Kier clearly found all of this strange and a shade excessive; we shall see in a moment more examples of Nazi authors who thought

American law went overboard. At any rate, what American law demonstrated, Kier wrote, was how natural and inevitable racist legislation was:

> This variegated abundance of statutory racial regulation in the States of the Union demonstrates that the elemental force of the necessity of segregating humans according to their racial descent makes itself felt even where a political ideology stands in the way—a political ideology that denies that human beings have different worth depending on their descent. A very brief overview of American race law is given by H. Krieger in the *Verwaltungsarchiv*.[150]

It was from there that Kier moved to his peroration, identifying America as Nazi Germany's forerunner despite its "liberal and democratic" ideology—as the country that had arrived at the "fundamental recognition" of the evils of race mixing, now to be carried to its logical fulfillment in the Third Reich.

Once again it is important to reject the idea that all this was somehow meant as mere propaganda, directed at foreign readers. Kier certainly did refer to international "misunderstanding" of the regime. But his chapter cannot have been meant for a foreign audience. This was another dense text in *Fraktur*, probably with limited foreign circulation,[151] intended to guide and inspire domestic Nazi deliberations. We should hear, in Kier's reference to the outside world, not an exercise in propaganda, but a kind of honest bewilderment about foreign "misunderstandings" of a scheme that was very close indeed to what was found in the United States. And we must remember that the Nazi regime, at the time, was not preaching extermination. What it was preaching arguably *did* represent a logical extension of much of American race law, much though we may want to pretend otherwise.

EVALUATING AMERICAN INFLUENCE

Like American immigration and citizenship law, American miscegenation law was thus a regular point of reference during the years when the Nuremberg Laws emerged. The question remains whether we can say that the Nazis were in some meaningful way directly "influenced" by American miscegenation practice. The answer to that question is an (inevitably controversial) yes.

First of all it is essential to reject once and for all the proposition that American law could not have been of interest to the Nazis because it did not expressly target Jews. The absence of Jews from American prohibitions did not deter Nazi jurists from investigating American law in the least. Yes, it is true that American antimiscegenation law primarily spoke of "Negroes" and "Mongols." But that hardly meant that American law had nothing to offer. Helmut Nicolai, the Nazi race fanatic with whom this chapter began, declared, in a major 1933 speech, that "Negroes" and "Mongols" represented a threat to racial purity just as Jews did,[152] and the Prussian Memorandum spoke, in the same vein, not just of Jews, but of "Jews, *Negroes or other coloreds*."[153] Radical Nazis throughout the early years of the 1930s were well aware that there was an American model to exploit, and they were quite willing to draw on American law in planning their "fundamental constitutional law of the national socialist state" on interbreeding and sex. It is simply nonsense to claim that Nazi lawyers could not have made use of American precedents because of the absence of formal measures against American Jews. These were able lawyers, who were quite capable of extracting legal techniques from statutes with goals somewhat different from their own.

Once we dispose of that dubious claim, we can indeed, and really must, speak frankly of something that can only reasonably be called "influence," as objectionable as that term is sure to seem. First and foremost, we can detect something that it is entirely right to deem "influence" in the criminalization of racially mixed marriages. The Blood Law decreed both the civil invalidity and the criminality of mixed marriages:

Law on the Protection of German Blood and German Honor

§ 1

(1) Marriages between Jews and nationals of German blood or racially related blood are forbidden. If such marriages are nevertheless entered into they are null and void, even if they are concluded abroad in order to evade this law.

. . .

§ 5

(1) Any person who violates the prohibition of § 1 shall be punished by imprisonment at hard labor.

The language of this law was certainly not directly copied from some American statute, but that is not the point. Legal influence on jurists as sophisticated as the Germans of the mid-twentieth century does not involve literal copying. Lawyers make use of larger conceptual frameworks while drafting language that suits their particular circumstances, and in this case the leading German lawyers of the early Nazi period framed their conceptual question as the question of whether marriage could ever be the subject of criminal law, outside the cases of bigamy and "malicious deception." American law offered the great example of a Western system that criminalized mixed marriages. German jurists had known that since the early twentieth century, they still knew it in the early 1930s, and they discussed the American sources in detail, both in print and in the critical closed-door meeting for which we possess a transcript. In particular, the radical Nazi Freisler, who pushed for broad criminalization from the Prussian Memorandum on, appears in that transcript as a vocal champion of American legislation and jurisprudence.

Skeptics may retort that Nazi radicals would have succeeded in criminalizing racially mixed marriages even if they had not had an American example to cite. That is perfectly possible; we will never know. Nevertheless there can be no justification for ignoring the evidence of Nazi engagement with American models that litters the sources. Even if the radicals were destined to win, that does not mean that having an American model meant nothing in the political battles of the early 1930s; nor that the radicals who cited American law over and over again were not in some significant way inspired by what they found. Only a naive and pedestrian understanding of law—only a dogged refusal to face facts—would dismiss the American example as insignificant in this setting. If we had evidence of this kind for any less freighted case in comparative law, we would not hesitate for a moment to speak of "influence." Konrad Zweigert and Hein Kötz, the preeminent postwar German specialists on comparative law, give a standard account of how foreign law affects legislative innovation:

> Legislators all over the world have found that on many matters good laws cannot be produced without the assistance of comparative law, whether in the form of general studies or of reports specially prepared on the topic in question.

> Ever since the second half of the nineteenth century legislation in Germany has been preceded by extensive comparative legal research.[154]

Like other postwar German scholars, Zweigert and Kötz pass over the Nazi period in silence; but their description of how laws are made is equally applicable to Germany in the period 1933 to 1935; it is just as pertinent to the making of bad laws as it is to the making of good ones; and the "extensive comparative research" conducted by the Nazi lawyers of the early 1930s inescapably links America to the making of the Nuremberg Laws.

DEFINING "MONGRELS": THE ONE-DROP RULE AND THE LIMITS OF AMERICAN INFLUENCE

America's role is clearest in the case of the criminalization of racially mixed marriages, but the American example also mattered for Nazi discussions of the classification of racially inferior "mongrels." American law was concerned with defining "Negroes" just as German law was concerned with defining "Jews," and Nazi observers were well aware that the United States offered a possible model. Lawyers were by no means the only Germans intrigued by American racial classification schemes. For example, there was this passage in a 1934 book that was published as a guide for teachers on how to present Nazi race policies to their pupils. The author observed that Americans took the need for racial purity so seriously that they were prepared to take what even Nazis regarded as exceedingly harsh classificatory measures: "Sharp social race separation of whites and blacks has shown itself to be necessary in the United States of America, even if it leads in certain cases to human hardness, as when a mongrel of predominantly white appearance is nevertheless reckoned among the niggers."[155] This was the world of the American one-drop rule, disturbing even to Nazi commentators, who shuddered at the "human hardness" it entailed. Another Nazi author, this time in an article written for English teachers in 1936, had similar words. He praised the American commitment to legislating racial purity, but he too blanched at "the unforgiving hardness of the social usage according to which an American man or woman who has even a drop of Negro blood in their veins," counted as blacks.[156]

The one-drop rule was too harsh for the Nazis (or at least for most of them—the fanatical Achim Gercke was in favor of something like it),[157] and for that reason alone the influence of American classification schemes was inevitably limited. The scholars who see parallels between American and Nazi racial classification schemes are to that extent wrong—but only because they understate the relative severity of American law.[158] The Nazi literature saw other obstacles as well. German Jews were simply not American blacks. American blacks, as one anonymous author explained in 1935, were generally physically recognizable as such, and that meant that America could rely on "mostly clear color lines."[159] Identifying Jews was far tougher. Unlike blacks, Jews maintained their communal identity by their culture, not their color. American blacks by contrast had lost all of their distinctive culture after centuries of oppression: "The Negroes [having lost their cultural traditions] are now held together only negatively, by their identifying physical features. . . . What the Jews and the Negroes of the USA have in common, however, is the will to become outwardly assimilated. In this regard the prospects of the Jews are seemingly better, since the bodily differences do not stand out visibly as strongly, and accordingly can be hidden more successfully."[160] Germany's "Jewish problem" was far more insidious than America's "Negro problem": the German Jews, this author worried, would find it all too easy to infiltrate themselves into the community by pretending to embrace the German characteristics of "diligence, love of orderliness, and thrift."[161]

America was different: there were limits to the possible extent of American influence on Nazi racial classifications, and Nazi authors were quite conscious of them. Nevertheless American racial classifications were of inevitable legal interest; that was a large part of the appeal in American miscegenation law. We see that in Justice Minister Gürtner's report on how American law defined the races. We see it in the *Handbook* article on "*Volk*, Race and State," carefully listing for its Nazi readership which American states defined blacks as those with which fraction of black blood. We see it in Johann von Leers's 1936 review of the laws of the American states.[162] We see it in Krieger's 1934 article, and later in his 1936 book.

And at least one aspect of American law may have carried some weight in the German debates: American states did not define "mongrels" strictly on the basis of descent. As Krieger explained, race classifications in the United States might also turn on other factors: The courts of some American states, in particular North Carolina and Texas, also looked to other "outward characteristics." Texas in particular considered marital history: "[O]utward characteristics [may] be decisive in determining membership in this or that population group, e.g., former slave status (North Carolina), the fact of regular social association with one or another group (ditto) or, in the case of a second marriage, the racial identity of the first marital partner (Texas)."[163]

The idea that race classifications might turn on something other than descent, and in particular on marital history, deserves to be flagged: that idea was of critical importance in the ultimate Nazi definition of "Jews." As we have seen, radicals wished to define Jews as those with only a single Jewish grandparent—the equivalent of what American states would call "1/4" colored. As early as April 1933, however, there was a counterproposal on the table. This alternative classification scheme proposed to spare half Jews—unless those half Jews either practiced the Jewish religion or entered into a marriage with a Jew.[164] It was that counterproposal that ultimately made its way into the crucial implementation ordinance of the Nuremberg Laws:[165]

First Regulation Issued Pursuant to the Reich Citizenship Law, November 14, 1935

§ 5 (1): A person *is* a Jew, if he descends from at least three grandparents who are racially full Jews.

(2) A person *counts* as a Jew, if he is a mongrel descended from two fully Jewish grandparents,

(a) who at the time of the promulgation of this law belongs to the Jewish religious community or is subsequently accepted into it, [or]

(b) who at the time of the promulgation of this law was married to a Jew or subsequently married a Jew.

[minor other provisions follow][166]

Thus the moderates managed to shield some, but only some, half Jews. Lösener justified this compromise by holding that life choices were relevant because they revealed the "inclinations" of the "mongrel" in question. The half Jews who "counted" as "Jews" were the ones who were not submitting to German cultural values: "Also reckoned among the Jews are certain *groups of half Jews* (persons with two full Jewish and two non-Jewish or not full Jewish grandparents), who on account of certain circumstances must be regarded as more strongly inclined toward Jewdom."[167] Did the American example count for something here? Krieger's article was not the only possible source for the notion that a juristic solution to the problem of classifying Jews might turn in part on marital history. As we have seen, the Nazi literature on American immigration law praised the American Cable Act rule denaturalizing women who stooped to marry Asian men.[168] It may have mattered, in the charged debates of the weeks after the promulgation of the Nuremberg Laws, that America, the model of a country with anti-miscegenation law, offered some support for the notion that marital history should play a role in assigning persons to one racial category rather than another.

In the end though we do not know. We cannot say what part if any this aspect of the American model played in German thinking. The bottom line is that the Nazis regarded American classification schemes as too harsh, and the American race problem as too different, for any unmodified borrowing to have taken place. But what ultimately matters is that they knew that there *was* an American example, and indeed the example that they turned to first, and over and over again.

CONCLUSION

AMERICA THROUGH NAZI EYES

On September 23, 1935, eight days after the Führer's proclamation of the Nuremberg Laws at the "Party Rally of Freedom," a delegation of forty-five Nazi lawyers gathered on board the luxury ocean liner SS *Europa*, bound for the United States on a "study trip" organized by the Association of National Socialist German Jurists. The group was led by Dr. Ludwig Fischer, at the time a high official in the Nazi Office of Legal Affairs. Four years later, Fischer would be named governor of the Warsaw District in Nazi-occupied Poland. There he would serve as the top functionary during the brutal roundup of hundreds of thousands of Polish Jews; the creation of the Warsaw Ghetto (in which, he promised, "the Jews will croak from hunger and misery. There will be nothing left of the Jewish problem but the cemetery");[1] the eventual savage suppression of the Warsaw Ghetto uprising; and the deportation of some three hundred thousand to the death camps.[2]

In September 1935, however, all that lay in the future. The forty-five Nazi lawyers who gathered on board the *Europa* under Fischer's leadership, including thirty-eight men and seven women, were traveling in style: as the Nazi legal press observed, the US dollar, pummeled by New Deal monetary policies, was at an advantageously low exchange rate, and they could promise themselves a posh experience.[3] The "study trip" was to begin in New York, where the delegation was to be feted at a reception organized by the New York City Bar Association.[4] Thereafter, they were to enjoy an educational program offering "special insight into the workings of American legal and economic life through study and lectures [as well as] a broad overview of life in the New World in general." (Members of the Nazi Accountants' Association were also invited to participate, though there is no sign that any Nazi accountants joined the trip.)[5]

Before they sailed, the forty-five received a festive onboard "greeting" from party legal bigwig Hans Frank, communicated to them by Wilhelm Heuber, chief of the Nazi Jurists' Association. The greeting gave voice to what must have been a sense of triumph among Nazi lawyers in the aftermath of the Nuremberg Rally, with its elevation of the swastika and formal enactment of the party anti-Jewish program almost three years in the making. The participants were, in the jargon of the association, "upholders of German law," and Heuber described their trip as the reward for a year of struggles on behalf of a new order that had prevailed over its opposition: "As Dr. Heuber explained ... [t]hrough this study trip the upholder of German law would gain the necessary compensation for an entire year of work opposing an outdated type of jurist, always inclined to ignore the realities of life."[6] Even at the distance of eighty years, one can almost still hear the forty-five Nazis murmuring their satisfaction over the victories of the year, raising their glasses, and clicking their heels.

Not all went smoothly on the trip, however. The forty-five arrived in New York on September 26. That was two months to the day after a thousand anti-Nazi rioters had stormed the SS *Bremen*, the sister ship of the *Europa* on which they sailed, and three weeks after Manhattan Magistrate Louis Brodsky had delivered his incendiary opinion declaring the swastika to be a "black flag of piracy" and Nazism to be "an atavistic throwback to pre-medieval, if not barbaric, social and political conditions."[7] New York City was, in short, a hotbed of anti-Nazi sentiment, home to numerous "Jewish elements," and the visitors met with protests. After they were spotted in their garment district hotel greeting each other with "Heil Hitler!" and giving the Nazi salute, Jewish fur merchants organized a noisy demonstration against them that lasted a full six hours and required a substantial police presence.[8]

Fischer, the leader of the group, responded to this disturbance with memorable indignation. Jews, huffed Fischer, who was to be hanged for his war crimes in 1947, "were treated in a kindly and dignified fashion" in Nazi Germany:

> We came on a study trip to gain first-hand impressions of America, and our first impression is a bad one.... The impression of the City of New York was tremendous, but the other impression was bad. I realize that decent-minded Americans do not approve of this demonstration, and are very friendly and hospitable. What I saw of the demonstration was exclusively Jewish.
>
> Germany treats her guests well, and even Jewish guests are welcome. This Summer there were several international conferences in Germany with Jewish participants, and they were treated in a kindly and dignified fashion.[9]

Once he was done venting his spleen, though, Fischer emphasized that "the impression of New York City itself [is] powerful and overwhelming," and he added an expression of his "especial satisfaction" at the warm reception that the City Bar Association had given him and his fellow Nazis.[10]

Sadly it does not seem possible to learn more about how Fischer and his group fared on their study trip (though the curious will find online a film of what is probably Fischer's hanging).[11] But as we have seen, we can know a great deal about Nazi interest in American law during their previous "year of work opposing an outdated type of jurist." There was plenty about America that Nazi lawyers of the early 1930s rejected—especially about the liberal America of Louis Brodsky, the Jewish fur merchants of New York, and those who agreed with them. But there was also plenty that Nazis found to like. Fischer was not the first Nazi lawyer to distinguish between Jews and "decent-minded Americans"; Hitler and Göring had done the same at the Nuremberg Rally eleven days earlier, and Fischer's delegation was not the first Nazi group to study America, nor the first to take away a powerful impression.

From *Mein Kampf* onward, Nazi jurists and policy makers took a sustained interest in American race law. Especially during the early 1930s, the era of the making of the Nuremberg Laws, Nazis engaged in detailed study of American immigration law, American second-class citizenship law, and American anti-miscegenation and mongrel-ization law. Some of them saw attractions in the system of Jim Crow segregation. In particular, the Prussian Memorandum, the 1933 text that laid out the basic statement of the radical Nazi legal program, specifically invoked Jim Crow—though it proposed a more "lim-ited" version for Nazi Germany. Certain aspects of American race law struck Nazi observers as appealing: in particular, the exceptional American practice of harshly criminalizing interracial marriage lay in the background of the Blood Law. Other aspects, like the one-drop rule, struck them as excessively severe. Some of the more vi-cious Nazis, notably Roland Freisler, championed the lessons to be learned from American legislation and jurisprudence, while moder-ates like Justice Minister Gürtner worked to downplay the useful-ness of American precedents. Nobody argued in favor of a wholesale importation of American practices; everybody was aware that Amer-ica had liberal traditions that were at war with its racism, but many expressed their approval of what the *National Socialist Handbook of Law and Legislation* called America's "fundamental recognition" of the imperative of creating a legally enforced race order—though Nazi authors always added that the task of building a fully realized race state remained for National Socialist Germany to complete.

What shall we say about all of this?

It is important to begin by underlining what the history in this book does not tell us: It does not explain the genesis of Nazism. No sensible person would conclude that it was American inspiration that led causally to the crimes of the Nazis. It is lunacy to claim, as extremists on both the left and right have been known to do, that the United States is the source of all evil in the world, and it would be lunacy to hold the United States responsible for what happened in Germany and its dominions from 1933 to 1945. Nazism happened for countless reasons, most of them indigenous to Germany; the responsibility for Nazi crimes rests with Germans and their direct collaborators. In the end the United States certainly played its part in the defeat of Hitler, and it has certainly been a force for good in the world often enough.

What the history presented in this book demands that we confront are questions not about the genesis of Nazism, but about the character of America. The Nazis, let us all agree, would have committed monstrous crimes regardless of how intriguing and attractive they found American race law. But how did it come to pass that America produced law that seemed intriguing and attractive to Nazis?

In some ways, that question is not hard to answer. We all know that there was racism in the United States, and that it ran deep. It is not news that America had ugly race law in the early twentieth century. We all already knew that there were parallels between Jim Crow America and Nazi Germany; after all, they are obviously there.[12] We already knew about the Nazi interest in American eugenics. Historians have already documented Nazi admiration for American westward expansion. If the Nazi vogue for Franklin Roosevelt is not well known, it has nevertheless been identified already. If we were not aware of the depth of Nazi interest in American race law during the making of the Nuremberg Laws, we should not be entirely astonished by it. The image of America as seen through

Nazi eyes in the early 1930s is not the image we cherish, but it is hardly unrecognizable.

Nevertheless, seeing America through Nazi eyes does tell us things we did not know, or had not fully reckoned with—things about the nature and dimensions of American racism, and things about the place of America in the larger world history of racism. Not least, seeing America through Nazi eyes tells us some uncomfortable things about the character of American legal culture.

AMERICA'S PLACE IN THE GLOBAL HISTORY OF RACISM

First of all, seeing America through Nazi eyes brings home a truth that wise scholars have recognized, but that our general culture has so far been slow to grasp. The history of American racism is not just a history of the Jim Crow South.[13] We must overcome the tendency to equate race law in America with the law of segregation; we must look beyond the "mirror images" of Nazi Germany and the southern states. If we think of the history of race in America as the history of *Plessy v. Ferguson* and *Brown v. Board of Education*, of segregation and the heroics of the civil rights movement, we risk blinding ourselves to an immense expanse of what has taken place. European observers of the 1930s all recognized that black-white conflict was only one aspect of the history of American racism.[14] Indeed, Nazis almost never mentioned the American treatment of blacks without also mentioning the American treatment of other groups, in particular Asians and Native Americans: To them what "Nordic" America faced was not just the "Negro problem," but the problems of "Mongols," of Indians, of Filipinos, and of innumerable other non-"Nordic" groups trying to "push their way in."[15] By the same token, America's influential stature in twentieth-century world racism had to do with wider American campaigns and other American forms of law than just segregation in the South. In particular, it had to do with national and nation-wide programs of race-based immigration, race-based second-class citizenship, and race-based anti-miscegenation law. Those were the aspects of American law that appealed most to Nazi Germany, not Jim Crow segregation in the narrow sense.

And as we have seen the appeal of those aspects of American law for the Nazis was strong. That is the unpleasant fact of the matter, and it forces us to confront an unpleasant historical datum about the place of America in the world history of racism: In the early twentieth century the United States was not just a country with racism. It was *the* leading racist jurisdiction—so much so that even Nazi Germany looked to America for inspiration. What David Fitzgerald and David Cook-Martin conclude about immigration—that "[t]he United States was the leader in developing explicitly racist policies of nationality and immigration"[16]—is true of the other areas of the law this book has surveyed as well. In the early twentieth century the United States, with its deeply rooted white supremacy and its vibrant and innovative legal culture, was the country at the forefront of the creation of racist law. That is how the Nazis saw matters, and they were not the only ones. The same was true in Brazil,[17] just as it was true in Australia and South Africa,[18] just as it was true of the German colonial administrators who went hunting for a model for the making of anti-miscegenation law.[19] And while the Nazis liked to mention South Africa as a fellow traveler, in practice they found very little South African law to cite in the early 1930s.[20] Their overwhelming interest was in the "classic example," the United States of America.

To be sure, to say that the United States was the leader in racist law-making is not to say that it was the only country that can be accused of racism. It most certainly was not. Europe had its own centuries-old history of persecution, which manifestly prefigured much of

Nazi policy: the Nazis of the early 1930s were not the first Europeans to seek to expel their Jews, as they were well aware.[21] Moreover there was race law of some kind to be found throughout the world of European colonial and imperial expansion. Iberia and Latin America had a tradition to which some historians trace the roots of modern race law, a tradition as old as the sixteenth century.[22] By the end of the nineteenth century there was explicitly race-based exclusionary immigration legislation in Brazil,[23] and a figure like Johann von Leers, Nazi author of *Blood and Race: A Tour through the History of Peoples*, was eager to argue that some measure of racist law could be found throughout the centuries.[24]

Most especially there was plenty of racism among the other daughter nations of British imperialism. We must pay attention when a leading Nazi jurist like Otto Koellreutter speaks of the "interesting results" to be found in "the United States and the British Dominions." Passages like that one suggest a haunting question about the Anglo-American, common-law world. The backdrop to Nazism is to be sought partly in British traditions: it is to be sought among the democracies of English-speaking "free white men" not only in America, but also in Australia, in South Africa, and to a lesser extent elsewhere on the British globe. These were all places where yeoman settlers claimed rights of egalitarian self-government at the expense of disfavored, and sometimes warred-upon, minorities,[25] and the Nazis looked with interest on all of them.

But within that world America was the leader during the age of the rise of Hitler. That is the truth, and we cannot squirm away from it. It was American immigration, citizenship, and anti-miscegenation law that the Nazis cited over and over again. It was American Jim Crow that was highlighted by the Prussian Memorandum. It was a memorandum on American law that the Justice Ministry prepared for discussion at the planning meeting of June 5, 1934. It was American law to which the radicals at that meeting turned. It was the American criminalization of racially mixed marriage that was the forerunner of the Blood Law. It was the American conquest of the West that Nazis invoked so often while engaged in the murderous campaigns of the 1940s, just as Hitler was already invoking it in the 1920s.[26] Nazism was certainly not a product made in America and imported into Germany, but it remains the case that when the Nazis set out to build a racist order, they turned to America first to see what sort of models they could find.

✳

Of course that sounds extremely strange today, and even perverse. We think of America as the home of liberty and equality, and as a stalwart in the herculean allied anti-Nazi struggles of World War II. More broadly we think of British common-law traditions as a prime historical source of the modern culture of rights, perhaps even as *the* prime historical source. But some of the strangeness dissipates once we understand the claims of Nazism. Nazism too was a movement for equality, if not for liberty: as I have argued elsewhere, the promise of the "National Revolution" of Nazism to the general German population was a promise of leveling up—a promise that all racial Germans as the Nazis defined them would count as high-status members of German society. Society would no longer be divided into noble Germans and commoner Germans, master Germans and servant Germans. Now every German would count as a coequal member of the ruling class by simple virtue of membership in the Master Race.[27] The Nazi "National Revolution" was in that sense a thoroughly egalitarian social revolution.

The resemblances to the Anglophone, and especially American, world were much less remote than we would suppose today. American white supremacy too was founded in a "resolute egalitarianism among white men";[28] it was a movement that affirmed the equality of every member of the favored race, while forcefully rejecting the status inequalities of the aristocratic past. Such was the nature of Jacksonian democracy in particular. In that sense the connection between American egalitarianism and American racism ran deep. When Hitler praised America in *Mein Kampf* it was partly because he believed that America permitted exactly the sort of leveling he believed Germany needed: America, unlike Europe, was producing a "wealth of inventions" because the Americans, unlike the Europeans, gave "talented people from the lowest social orders" the chance to make something of themselves.[29] Hitler too promised to transform German society by bringing "people from the lowest social orders" up in the world. Of course this egalitarian promise could be realized only at the expense of non-"Aryans," but again this was nothing different from what was to be found in vast stretches of the Anglophone world. In this connection it is worth observing that the German words for "master," *Herr*, and "supremacy," *Vorherrschaft* or *Oberherrschaft*, are close cognates: the German "Master Race" is the near linguistic cousin of the English "white supremacy," and German authors of the Nazi period understood it that way.

So the Nazi interest in America in the 1930s is not quite as strange as it seems today. It is also of course essential to bear in mind the geopolitics of the age. The Nazis looked out on a globe that had been largely mastered by English-speaking countries. The British had aimed for world domination long before Hitler did.[30] Moreover Anglo-American leaders and intellectuals themselves, most prominent among them Teddy Roosevelt and James Bryce, explained and defended their control of so much of the earth with frankly racist arguments; these were men who believed, in the words of TR, in keeping "the temperate zones of the new and the newest worlds a heritage for the white people."[31] And among the "Nordic" powers, America was the natural geopolitical model for Nazi Germany, as scholars have rightly noted. It was the "Anglo-Saxon" United States that had built an imposing continental empire, and that therefore stood out as an expansionist model for the Reich that was determined to conquer to its east. It was the "Anglo-Saxon" United States that had invented an international law doctrine that justified its place as a hegemon in its hemisphere, in the form of the Monroe Doctrine and its more assertive Roosevelt Corollary of 1904.[32] To be sure, interwar German racists often speculated that the United States would succumb to race mixing and therefore decline—though Adolf Hitler himself thought differently, at least until the outbreak of World War II.[33] But even if some of them thought America might falter, that was no reason for them to refuse to learn the lessons of American racism. The possibility of American geopolitical decline only brought home the truth that Nazi Germany would have to apply American policies with a rigor that the Americans themselves had failed to sustain.

✦

But for all the attractions of "Nordic" America in Nazi Germany, is it not obvious that there remained significant, and ultimately profound, differences?

Of course there were, as the Nazis themselves emphasized. First and foremost, American race law coexisted with a constitutional tradition that had a strong grip on American legal culture, especially in the form of the Reconstruction Amendments. To be sure, that grip was not strong enough to prevent the United States from pioneering in the creation of racist institutions. American legal history of the decades after 1877 is a largely unrelieved record of shameful evasion of the principle of equality that the Reconstruction Amendments were supposed to enshrine[34]—the principle, as the Nazis contemptuously put it, "that everyone who bears a human countenance is equal." Nevertheless, the Reconstruction Amendments were there, and American lawyers always had to reckon with them, if only in devising evasions. As Desmond King and Rogers Smith have written, there was always a tension between two racial orders in America, a "white supremacist order" and an "egalitarian transformative order."[35] There was certainly nothing comparable in Nazi Germany, and Nazi observers looked on the American constitutional tradition with a mixture of bemusement and disdain.

Nor was it only the constitutional tradition that set America apart from Nazi Germany. There was also another, arguably even more important, difference as well: Nazi racists made a very different, and far more merciless, use of state power than American racists did. On this subject it is useful to turn to Gunnar Myrdal, the Swedish social scientist whose 1944 book *An American Dilemma: The Negro Problem and Modern Democracy* did so much to shake up American race relations and set the stage for the civil rights movement after World War II. Here is how Myrdal answered the question, commonplace in the 1930s and 1940s, of whether the Jim Crow South should be characterized as "fascist":

IS THE SOUTH FASCIST?

On account of the one-party system and the precarious state of civil liberties, the South is sometimes referred to as fascist. This is, however, wrong. . . . The South entirely lacks the centralized organization of a fascist state. Southern politics is, on the contrary, decentralized and often even chaotic. The Democratic party is the very opposite of a "state party" in a modern fascist sense. It has no conscious political ideology, no tight regional or state organization and no centralized and efficient bureaucracy. The "regimentation" which keeps the South politically solid is not an organization *for* anything—

least of all for a general policy—it is a regimentation *against* the Negro. The South is static and defensive, not dynamic and aggressive.[36]

There are things to object to in this analysis. Arguably the Southern Democratic Party *did* have a "general policy" in the early 1930s, when, as Katznelson argues, it provided critical political support for the New Deal, and especially for anti-poverty government programs for its impoverished region.[37] And the Nazi variant of fascism certainly was very much directed *against* Jews, not just *for* some positive vision. The resemblance between the United States and Nazi Germany in the early 1930s is closer than Myrdal allows.

Still, at the end of the day Myrdal put his finger on what is arguably the single most important difference between the racism in the Nazi mode and racism among their "tribally related Americans." There was American, and more broadly Anglophone, racism in the background to the Nazi movement, but the Nazis brought something different: the "organization of a fascist state." It is indeed the case that America was (and is) "decentralized and . . . chaotic" by contrast with what emerged in the Central Europe of Hitler; America did indeed (and does) lack a "centralized and efficient bureaucracy." The contrast emerges repeatedly in this book. We have seen how the Nuremberg Laws were intended to institute official state persecution in order to displace street-level lynchings; the United States by contrast remained faithful to lynch justice. (Indeed, the number of lynchings rose noticeably during the period 1933 to 1935.)[38] We have seen that the United States, in its immigration and citizenship law, held back from open state-decreed racism, trusting instead in the legal subterfuges and covert devices necessary to preserve the façade of compliance with the Fourteenth Amendment. The Nazis by contrast decreed their racism openly. The Nazis saw a great deal to like in America's "fundamental recognition" of the necessity of a race-based order, but they set out to make the creation of their own race-based order the business of an efficient state apparatus of a kind Americans have always refused to tolerate.

So the differences were there, and they were real; nobody should conclude that Nazism was some sort of mechanical transplantation of American racism into the soil of Central Europe. But the similarities were there too, and we cannot wish them away. There were reasons why Nazi observers could arrive at appalling judgments such as that our Founding had created "the strongest prop" in "the struggle of the Aryans for world domination."[39] There were reasons why the *National Socialist Monthly* could write so warmly, in November 1933, that "to tribally related Americans we reach out our hand in friendship."[40] White supremacy did indeed have a storied history in America, as a matter of legal history dating back at least to 1691, when Virginia adopted America's first race-based anti-miscegenation statute, and to 1790, when the First Congress chose to open naturalization to "any alien, being a free white person." In the early years of the 1930s, moreover, American white supremacy stood at one of its high-water marks, as the early New Deal did its work in political dependence on the Democratic Party that ruled in the South.

When we add it all up, the right conclusion is this: American white supremacy, and to some extent Anglophone white supremacy more broadly, provided, to our collective shame, some of the working materials for the Nazism of the 1930s. In that sense the history of Nazism cannot be fully told without a chapter on the "interesting results" that Otto Koellreutter identified in "the United States and the British Dominions." But in Nazi Germany supremacist traditions and practices acquired the backing of a state apparatus far more powerful than anything to be found in the world of the daughters of British Imperialism, and far more ruthless than any that had ever existed in Europe west of the Elbe.

NAZISM AND AMERICAN LEGAL CULTURE

The questions that must be addressed are not just about American and Anglophone white supremacy. There are also questions about the pragmatic American style of common-law jurisprudence that Freisler touted to his Nazi colleagues as one that "would suit us perfectly." The allure of American race law was not just the allure of a "Nordic" continental empire dedicated to white supremacy. It was also the allure of an open-ended, flexible, American common-law approach to the law. It was the allure of American "realism," an approach to the law that was prevalent among leading Nazi lawyers just as it was among leading lawyers of the New Deal. Not least it was the allure of the kind of American willingness to innovate that continues to make us global leaders in many areas of the law today, just as it made us the leaders in eugenics and race legislation a century ago. What attracted Nazi lawyers was not just American racism but American legal culture, and that means that we must face some uncomfortable questions about the value of the American way of doing things.

Some of the most striking, and inescapable, questions have to do with the common-law tradition. What Freisler admired about American law is manifestly the same thing that we often celebrate in the common-law tradition today: the common law's flexibility and open-endedness, and the adaptability to "changing societal requirements" that its judge-centered, precedent-based approach is often said to permit.[41] Other Nazis too had admiring things to say about American judge-made common law, which, they declared, had facilitated the creation of a healthy law that "emerged out of the *Volk*" rather than being the product of barren legal formalism.[42] What should we think about this?

The question is especially pressing because it has become so com-monplace in America these days to celebrate the common law as superior—and superior precisely because it is thought to embody what Friedrich Hayek, the great Austrian champion of free markets, and a man shut out from his home country by Nazism, called "the constitution of liberty." American authors today frequently contrast the liberty-oriented virtues of the common law with the defects of the code-based civil-law tradition of continental Europe, which they view as overly rigid—a system in which the law is reduced to the comparatively inflexible commands of a powerful state. Here is how a leading American law professor explains why, of the two, the com-mon law is today so widely regarded as embodying superior values:

> Hayek provides the most prominent discussion . . . of differ-ences between legal families. He argues vigorously that the English legal tradition (the common law) is superior to the French (the civil law), not because of substantive differences in legal rules, but because of differing assumptions about the roles of the individual and the state. In general, Hayek believed that the common law was associated with fewer government restrictions on economic and other liberties. . . . These views are correct as a matter of legal history.[43]

The comparative freedom of the common-law judge, on this account, is the institutional expression of a grander culture of common-law liberty, to be contrasted with the comparative subjection of the citi-zens of continental Europe and the comparative unfreedom of the civil-law jurist, bound to follow the positive commands of the state embodied in the code.[44] Common-law judicial authority is a bul-wark against excessive state power. This conception of the common law is not always articulated with perfect clarity, but it seems fair to say that it is broadly, if vaguely, embraced in America today. Indeed it occupies a place somewhere in the core of our understanding of the nature of American liberty. It certainly leaves one wondering why any Nazis would ever have had anything good to say about the American common law.

At the same time there is a widespread belief that Nazism was facilitated by precisely the sort of state-heavy positivism that Hayek feared and denounced. To be a Nazi, it is assumed, was to submit unconditionally to the will of the Führer, surrendering all powers of independent judgment; it was to have a law without liberty. The Nazi philosophy of law, on this view, was a crass version of what philosophers call "legal positivism": it was a philosophy that reduced law to the bare command of the sovereign/dictator; it was a philosophy of "subservience"[45] and obedience;[46] and the lesson of the crimes of Nazism is a lesson about the dangers of state-heavy positivistic approaches, which threaten, at the limit, to reduce all of society to serfdom.

Yet the history that I have recounted in this book suggests clearly enough that something more complicated was going on; and so it was. In fact careful students of Nazism have demonstrated that the legal philosophy that prevailed under Hitler was not a philosophy of crass legal positivism at all.[47] What the Nazis espoused was something much closer to what Freisler espoused: it was something close to common-law pragmatism, and if there are jurisprudential lessons to be learned from the crimes of Nazism they are not lessons in any simple way about the dangers of crass legal positivism or of civil-law attitudes.

For the striking truth is that Nazi jurists were opposed to any theory of the law that reduced it to mere obedience. Yes it is the case that Germany was to be ruled by the *Führerprinzip*, the doctrine of obedience to the leader. But while it is true that ordinary citizens were to be blindly obedient, Nazi officials were expected to take a different attitude. Nazi teachings on this score can be found, for example, in an early version of the Oath to Adolf Hitler from 1934, produced by his right-hand man Rudolf Hess: According to the oath, while ordinary Germans were to swear to obey the commands of the Führer unconditionally, "political leaders" were enjoined "to be loyal to the spirit of Hitler. Whatever you do, always ask: How would the *Führer* act, in accordance with the image you have of him."[48] This was a formula for a real discretion in pursuing Nazi goals. As Ian Kershaw puts it, officials were to "work towards the Führer."[49] Yes it is the case that the Nazis vested limitless power in the "centralized organization of a fascist state." But they rejected the idea that the officials who wielded that authority should be mere foot soldiers, deprived of individual initiative. If they denied the liberty of the ordinary German citizen, they frequently insisted on a kind of liberty for the individual Nazi official to act independently "in the spirit of Hitler." That is indeed a part of what made Nazism so terrifying.

And yes it is the case that Nazism emerged in a continental Europe with a code-based civil-law tradition. But it would be utterly mistaken to imagine that the Nazis embraced or embodied that civil-law tradition. On the contrary, the critical truth of legal history is that the Nazis set out to smash the traditional juristic attitudes of the civil-law jurist. Far from representing the traditions of the legalistic state, the Nazis belonged to a culture of contempt for the ways continental lawyers had been trained to work. Nazi radicals understood themselves to be, in the words of Hans Frank's "greeting" to the forty-five lawyers who gathered on the SS *Europa* in September 1935, a movement that opposed the "outdated type of jurist, always inclined to ignore the realities of life," and that meant that they were steadfastly opposed to the traditions of the civil law as they had existed in Germany before the Nazi takeover of the German state.

We see the resulting conflict playing itself out in the June 5, 1934, meeting. Franz Gürtner, Bernhard Lösener, Hans von Dohnanyi, and the other advocates of relative moderation in the persecution of the Jews represented precisely the "outdated type of jurist" that radicals like Freisler were determined to shoulder aside, and if we are to understand the jurisprudential drama of the clash at the meeting, and the appeal of the American common-law approach for a man like Freisler, it is imperative that we describe their attitudes with more care and sympathy than a Friedrich Hayek could muster. As we have seen, these civil-law jurists were men who thought of the law as a science. That science had established a body of basic rules that set real limits on what jurists, or for that matter legislators, could do; legislators could no more ignore the logical dictates of legal science than they could repeal the laws of gravity or mathematics. The radical Nazi program of the Prussian Memorandum in particular could not be coherently incorporated into the edifice of criminal law, and for that reason it had to be rejected, or at the very least drastically modified.

This avowedly "scientific" attitude is the true mark of the well-trained jurist in the civil-law tradition. It is certainly different from the attitude of the common-law judge, but it is not an attitude of meek submissiveness to the state. On the contrary, we can think of this juristic commitment to the "science" of the law as imposing quasi-constitutional limits on any radical legislative program. The traditions of legal science constituted, as it were, the code in which legislation had to be written. The consequence, even as late as the early summer of 1934, was that the "scientifically" informed legal profession was in a position to ride herd on the demands of Nazi radicals, much though those radicals might push for "political" or "primitive" rather than "scientific" decisions. Yes, the state in the civil-law world was in principle comparatively powerful, but the traditions of legal science operated to keep it in check.

A man like Freisler was drawn to American jurisprudence precisely because it was not hobbled by this sort of "outdated" respect for legal science and juristic tradition; and that ought to be enough to raise doubts in our minds about whether common-law liberty offers the best defense against tyranny of the Nazi kind. Common-law America attracted Roland Freisler because, in his Nazi eyes, ours was a country that enjoyed the blessings of liberty from the straitjacket of formalistic legal science, and by German standards he was right: America was, and is, a country where belief that there are "scientific" principles of the law that impose limits on what politics can do has always been comparatively weak. Trained "legal scientists" have never wielded the kind of power in America that Gürtner and Lösener were still able to wield in early June 1934.

To be sure, Americans have certainly sometimes cultivated something that they have called "legal science,"[50] and the American version of legal science has certainly sometimes imposed limits on the legislative process. In the late nineteenth and early twentieth centuries in particular, self-described American "legal scientists" dominated institutions like the Harvard Law School. During the same period the Supreme Court developed its own "legal science," founded in the Due Process Clause of the Fourteenth Amendment, which it used to strike down progressive economic legislation, most famously in the 1905 case *Lochner v. New York.*[51] To some extent American lawyers of what is commonly called the "*Lochner* era" aspired to claim the same authority that German "legal scientists" like Gürtner and Lösener aspired to claim.

But if Americans sometimes liked to speak of their "legal science," the reality is that American legal science was always a far weaker force than German legal science. The doctrinal "legal science" of American law schools was never a match for the subtlety and systematic depth of its German counterpart. As for the *Lochner* era courts, while they sometimes struck down economic legislation, they also left much progressive legislative untouched. More importantly they left racist legislation almost entirely untouched as well. When it came to race, American "legal science" generally yielded unceremoniously to American politics.[52] As for American common-law judges, unlike German "legal scientists" such as Lösener they showed no sign of concern about the conceptual incoherence of their racist decisions. Where Lösener insisted that criminalization was at best problematic in the absence of a scientifically defensible definition of a "Jew," American common-law judges, as Freisler approvingly noted, simply improvised their conceptions of "coloreds" as they went along.

That was the racist America that commanded the respect of radical Nazi lawyers: it was an America where politics was comparatively unencumbered by law. The great jurisprudential conflict at work in Nazi Germany was not the conflict between common-law liberty and civil-law state power. The great conflict was between lawfulness, as founded in a civil-law idea of legal science, and lawlessness, in favor of which a man like Freisler could invoke the American common law.[53] Nazi law, as a man like Freisler imagined it, was not a crass form of legal positivism, reducing the law to a duty of obedience to the command of the superiors. Nazi law was law that was liberated from the juristic past—it was law that would free the judges, legislators, and party bosses of Nazi Germany from the shackles of inherited conceptions of justice, allowing them to "work toward" the realization of the racist goals of the regime, with a sense of their duty to use their discretion in the spirit of Adolf Hitler.[54] Judges in particular were to enjoy meaningful independence to be exercised in line with the goals of the Führer.[55] By this means, the law would institutionalize and perpetuate a savage form of national revolution, by giving discretion to the savage instincts of innumerable Hitlers in innumerable state offices. It would create a Nazi hydra. That is precisely how Freisler conducted himself in office as President of the People's Court. And that was why the jurisprudence of the common law, with its "pragmatism," its "immediacy," its surrender of lawmaking authority to the judges, attracted him so much.

✷

It is in light of the same issues, finally, that we should think about the nature of 1930s "realism."

It is a large part of the story that throughout the 1930s leading lawyers in both Nazi Germany and New Deal America were self-proclaimed "realists"—equally committed in both countries to combating the "outdated type of jurist, always inclined to ignore the realities of life." On the American side, this was the high age of the movement called American Legal Realism, which has long been described as one of the great products of an American pragmatic style, ready to tackle social problems in a can-do spirit and displaying a healthy resistance to dogmatism. Such realism, for its American supporters, was sharply opposed to "formalism," a style that produced a rigid kind of pseudo-scientific law unable to adapt to the modern social needs.[56] The association between this American Legal Realism and the New Deal is close indeed,[57] and American lawyers often express considerable pride in their realist tradition, "the most important indigenous jurisprudential movement in the United States," as Brian Leiter writes, "during the twentieth century."[58]

Meanwhile the economic programs of the early New Deal were undertaken in a closely related pragmatic spirit. As Franklin Roosevelt described the American mood in a famous 1932 speech, "the country demands bold, persistent experimentation."[59] The epic legal drama of the early 1930s, retold in every history of the New Deal, was the drama of the conflict between the bold experimenters of the administration and a hostile Supreme Court. Jack Balkin describes how the lawyers of the 1930s viewed this struggle. On one side there was a conservative Supreme Court with its history of striking down at least some progressive economic legislation on "formalistic" grounds. On the other side was New Deal "pragmatism," oriented toward "social realities": "[D]uring the 'Lochner Era' courts employed a rigid formalism that neglected social realities, while the New Deal engaged in a vigorous pragmatism that was keenly attuned to social and economic change. The Lochner Era Court imposed laissez-faire conservative values through its interpretations of national power and the Due Process Clause, while the New Deal brought flexible and pragmatic notions of national power that were necessary to protect the public interest."[60] The conservative Supreme Court famously continued to block the key reforms of the New Deal until the momentous "switch in time" of 1937, which at last put the Court behind the administration's program. This epic struggle between executive and judiciary, like other aspects of the New Deal, was followed in the Nazi literature, and Nazi authors saw it in the same terms that American realists did: the battle was precisely a test of whether the "bold experiments" of New Deal politics could overcome "outdated" legalistic conceptions of the dictates of the Constitution in favor of the necessary "realistic" action in the face of economic crisis. As one Nazi commentator put it, the Supreme Court's decisions striking down the programs of the early New Deal were "incomprehensibly formalistic and alien to life."[61]

Meanwhile, on the German side, anti-formalistic approaches dominated in Nazi writings during the same years as well, though Nazis did not use the term "realism" as frequently or consistently as Americans did. The Nazi jurists who participated would be among the most influential in Germany throughout the twentieth century—though after the war all of them made determined efforts to suppress the record of their Nazi activities; today there is little national German pride in that country's 1930s Nazi Realism.[62] Nevertheless there was indeed something it is reasonable to call 1930s Nazi Realism, and it was a vigorous movement. And it is a striking fact that when scholars set out to describe the jurisprudence of both the United States and Nazi Germany, they arrive at formulas that are almost identical. The American legal realists, we read, were driven by "the perception that law and life were out of sync";[63] in just the same way, we read that for the Nazis the great aim was "to overcome the alienation between life and law."[64] "Life-law before formal-law is the fundamental drive of national socialist legal life," as one Nazi put it.[65] Bringing law back in line with "life" and "social realities" was the watchword on both sides of the Atlantic in these troubled years.

So what precisely was the connection between the two "realisms," Nazi and New Deal? Certainly in the 1930s there were plenty of observers who thought the affinities were close. As G. Edward White has written, throughout the decade the American Legal Realists had to struggle with the "perceived relationship between their moral relativism and the rise of amoral totalitarian governments."[66] In April 1934, for example, Karl Llewellyn, the leading voice of American Legal Realism, was told that "you have been accepted as a true Nazi, fit to be amalgamated in the lifeblood of the new Reich." Llewellyn, who was an energetically committed liberal, responded with real anger,[67] but he was not the only figure who had to navigate the ugly associations of "realism" in the 1930s. Another noteworthy example is Hans Morgenthau, the pioneer of "realism" in international relations. Morgenthau had begun his career as a young lawyer in Germany, where he had imbibed the most advanced German legal thought of the Weimar Republic. With the coming of Hitler in the 1930s, though, he fled abroad, and as a freshly arrived exile in America, he decided he had to avoid the term "realism," as his biographer writes, "because he worried that it might encourage American readers to place him in the camp of American Legal Realism, or even worse, to infer an association with Nazi ideologues who were also advocating a 'realistic' view of the law."[68] It was not until after World War II that Morgenthau was willing to advocate "realism" again.

An odor of Nazism was clinging to our "most important indigenous jurisprudential movement" in the early 1930s. That certainly does not mean that the American Legal Realists were Nazi sympathizers. Most of them unquestionably were not. The Realists were not in reality fascists, any more than FDR was in reality a dictator.[69] The fact that there was a Nazi variant of Realism certainly does not imply that we must recoil in horror from everything in our own tradition. The American Legal Realist movement yielded some superb insights, from which there is still much to learn, in my view.[70] Moreover there is a case to be made that it was the American Legal Realism of the New Deal era that eventually set the stage for *Brown v. Board of Education* in the 1950s.[71] In any case, whatever resemblances there may have been, the fact remains that the Nazi courts descended into appalling depths of lawlessness. Even at their worst, American courts were better.[72] Nevertheless, for all that, there *were* unmistakable resemblances between New Deal Realism and Nazi Realism, and we cannot properly assess Nazi interest in American race law, and the Nazi sense of kinship with the United States in the early years of the Hitler regime, unless we make some effort to grapple with them.

There was more to "Realism" in New Deal America and Nazi Germany than I can explore here; the topic requires a book of its own. Here I would like to emphasize only the obvious point: The "realists" of both countries shared the same eagerness to smash the obstacles that "formalistic" legal science put in the way of "life" and politics—and "life" in both New Deal America and Nazi Germany did not include only economic programs designed to lift the two countries out of the Depression. "Life" also involved racism.

It is here that the affinities between the realisms of Nazi Germany and New Deal America should really begin to make us shift uneasily in our seats. American Legal Realism was not just the possession of liberals like Karl Llewellyn; there were also many prominent American racists of the 1930s who embraced it.[73] The "realistic" attitude in American law did not just involve yielding to political decision makers when it came to economic legislation; it was also involved yielding to political decision makers when it came to racist legislation. And while some prominent realists spoke out against American racism, during the 1930s, most passed over the race question in silence.[74] In that sense the American Legal Realism of the early 1930s was entirely at home in the early New Deal, founded as it was on the Mephistophelean bargain between economic reformers and southern racists. The same "realistic" legal philosophy that could be invoked to defend the "bold [economic] experiments" of FDR could also be invoked to defend the racism of the Southern Democratic Party.

Such was the American scene in the early years of Hitler's regime, as it presented itself to the eyes of German lawyers. America was a country that united economic reform, in the face of the Great Depression, with racism. The racist side of it was perceptively described by Heinrich Krieger, the former exchange student at the University of Arkansas Law School whose work made its way into the hands of the Ministry of Justice officials planning the Blood Law, the German lawyer whose research did the most to shape Nazi understandings of America. Krieger saw that the deep tension in American race law was no different from the deep tension in American economic law: as he put it, the United States was a country torn between the two "shaping forces" of formalism and realism. When it came to race in particular, there was on the one hand the formalistic jurisprudence of the Fourteenth Amendment, with its commitment, so "alien to life," to the equality of all human beings; and on the other hand the "realistic" racism of a law that was rooted in the "legal intuitions of the American *Volk*," and that had produced the ingenious "devious pathways" of second-class citizenship law alongside the frank racism of anti-miscegenation statutes.[75] Krieger did not think that this American state of affairs was healthy. He believed that America was struggling to be open about its legal racism, as it ought to be, but that it had not yet managed to do so. Nevertheless he remained hopeful that the United States might achieve full health once it finally abandoned its formalism in favor of its realism. One southern racist published a 1938 review of Krieger's book that communicated his hopes for America perfectly. *Race Law in the United States*, wrote the reviewer, was a "scholarly and valuable study," informed by Krieger's "realism." The Nazi Krieger was a "frank" man, "fac[ing] the problem squarely," and he made a powerful case for reviving the racial exclusionism of his heroes Jefferson and Lincoln: "Krieger is convinced by his studies—and he will convince any sincere reader as well—that our race problems can be solved only after we have found our way back to the point of view held by our greatest statesmen. That was a realistic point of view, and it alone can lead to a healthy and fair solution for all races concerned."[76] Such was the "realistic point of view" that Heinrich Krieger carried home from Fayetteville to Nazi Germany.

★

Perhaps it goes without saying that all this should give us a bit of pause when it comes to American legal culture, with its pragmatic traditions and the vaunted openness and adaptability of its common law. Sometimes the American common law may indeed produce superior results, with its comparatively underdeveloped attachment to "legal science," its experimental quality, and its liberal grant of authority to judges. American contract law, for example, is, in my view, exemplary in its innovativeness. Sometimes the American democratic political process produces admirable legislation. But to have a common-law system like that of America is to have a system in which the traditions of the law do indeed have little power to ride herd on the demands of the politicians, and when the politics is bad, the law can be very bad indeed.

The resulting dangers have not vanished, and it would be wrong to close this book without pointing to at least one contemporary realm of American law in which they are still making themselves felt. That realm is American criminal justice. American criminal justice is spectacularly, and frighteningly, harsh by international standards. It includes practices that are sometimes uncomfortably reminiscent of those introduced by the Nazis—for example "three-strikes-and-you're-out" laws, a form of habitual offender sentencing. The Nazis too promoted habitual offender sentencing.[77] What makes contemporary America so exceptionally harsh? The answer, in part, is that contemporary American criminal law is unique, in the advanced economic world, in the extent to which it is shaped by the political process, whether through tough-on-crime legislation, or through the election of judges and prosecutors, a practice unheard of in the rest of the world.[78] Conversely, American "legal science" has proven uniquely incapable of staving off the dangers of the politicization of criminal law over the past generation. American jurists do not have the influence to put the brakes on the projects of politicians who make their careers on tough-on-crime platforms; post-Nazi continental Europe, where the traditions of legal science have reasserted themselves powerfully, is different in this regard. In continental Europe today the legal profession generally manages to keep a steady hand on the criminal justice system.[79] Not so in the United States: what Roland Freisler saw, and admired, in American race law eighty years ago is still with us in the politics of American criminal justice—as is, not least, the American race problem that looms so large in it. The story in this book, in that sense, is not done yet.

★

"There is currently *one* state," wrote Adolf Hitler, "that has made at least the weak beginnings of a better order." When one thinks of race law, said Nazi lawyer and later SS-Obersturmbannführer Fritz Grau, one thinks of "North America." "It is attractive to seek foreign models," declared Reich Minister of Justice Franz Gürtner, and like others before them, it was American models that the lawyers of the ministry found. To be sure, America had failed to target the Jews "so far," as Heinrich Krieger acknowledged, but apart from that "exception," declared Roland Freisler, hanging judge of the National Socialist People's Court, America had things to teach Germany: The United States had produced an admirably uninhibited racist jurisprudence, a jurisprudence that did not trouble itself about juristic niceties and that would therefore "suit us perfectly." In the eyes of these Nazis, the United States was indeed the "classic example." It was the country that produced the really "interesting" innovations, the natural first place to turn for anybody in the business of planning a "race state." That is why the *National Socialist Handbook of Law and Legislation* could close its chapter on how to build a race state by describing America as the country that had achieved the "fundamental recognition" of the truths of racism, and taken the first necessary steps, now to be carried to fulfillment by Nazi Germany.

Yes, of course it is also true that the United States was, and remains, the pioneer of many magnificent legal institutions. Of course there were also many aspects of the liberal democratic tradition in America that the Nazis found contemptible. Of course

America proved a generous place of refuge for at least some of the victims of Nazism. Nevertheless when it came to race law, numerous Nazi lawyers regarded America as the prime exemplar; and, much though we may wish to deny it, it was not outlandish for them to think of their program of the early 1930s as a more thoroughgoing and rigorous realization of American approaches toward blacks, Asians, Native Americans, Filipinos, Puerto Ricans, and others— even if the regime had shifted its sights to a new target in the form of the Jews, even if it would later take the racist exercise of modern state power in an unimaginably horrifying new direction.

This too has to be a part of our national narrative.

ACKNOWLEDGMENTS

I began the research for this book at Princeton, where I had the luxury of being a 2014–15 fellow at the Program on Law and Public Affairs. I have since benefited from the support of the Oscar M. Ruebhausen Fund at Yale Law School. Several friends and colleagues gave me invaluable research advice and comments: In particular I would like to thank Ariela Gross, Daniel Sharfstein, Samuel Moyn, Patrick Weil, Vivian Curran, Kenneth Ledford, David Eng, Van Gosse, Dirk Hartog, Jacqueline Ross, David Schleicher, Bruce Ackerman, and Lawrence Friedman. Daniel Rodgers subjected an early version of the project to a bracingly tough and skeptical reading. I hope this version persuades him. I am especially grateful to Christoph Paulus, who not only gave me comments but took the time to review my translations. Mark Pinkert provided excellent research assistance on the history of American law and Jenny Wolkowicki was a sharp-eyed and supportive production editor. I profited from the comments of numerous workshop participants at Columbia Law School, Harvard Law School, Yale Law School, and the Buchmann Faculty of Law at Tel Aviv University. My thanks to all of them.

The book greatly benefited from the comments of three anonymous referees for Princeton University Press. Their thoughtful, learned, and occasionally suitably bilious responses made me glad that I chose to bring this project to an academic publisher.

Sara McDougall was my partner in this as in all things.

NOTES

NOTES TO INTRODUCTION

1. Johnpeter Horst Grill and Robert L. Jenkins, "The Nazis and the American South in the 1930s: A Mirror Image?," *Journal of Southern History* 58, no. 4 (November 1992): 667–94.

2. For discussion of the parallels, see George Fredrickson, *Racism: A Short History* (Princeton: Princeton University Press, 2002), 2, 129; Judy Scales-Trent, "Racial Purity Laws in the United States and Nazi Germany: The Targeting Process," *Human Rights Quarterly* 23 (2001): 259–307.

3. Mark Mazower, *Hitler's Empire: How the Nazis Ruled Europe* (New York: Penguin, 2008), 584, discussed more fully in Chapter 1. See also the clever speculations of a student paper published in 2002: Bill Ezzell, "Laws of Racial Identification and Racial Purity in Nazi Germany and the United States: Did Jim Crow Write the Laws That Spawned the Holocaust?," *Southern University Law Review* 30 (2002–3): 1–13.

4. Andreas Rethmeier, *"Nürnberger Rassegesetze" und Entrechtung der Juden im Zivilrecht* (New York: Lang, 1995), 138–39.

5. Ibid., 139.

6. Ibid.

7. Richard Bernstein, "Jim Crow and Nuremberg Laws," *H-Judaica*, March 31, 1999, http://h-net.msu.edu/cgi-bin/logbrowse.pl?trx=vx&list=H-Judaic&month=99 03&week=e&msg=BHhgu7G7S8og2GgfCEpHNg&user=&pw=.

8. *H-Judaica*, March 31, 1999, quoted in Bernstein, "Jim Crow and Nuremberg Laws."

9. Jens-Uwe Guettel, *German Expansionism, Imperial Liberalism, and the United States, 1776–1945* (Cambridge: Cambridge University Press, 2012), 204–6.

10. Rethmeier, *"Nürnberger Rassegesetze,"* 140. For a similar assessment, with interesting additional material on Nazi references to the United States, see Michael Mayer, *Staaten als Täter. Ministerialbürokratie und "Judenpolitik" in NS-Deutschland und Vichy Frankreich. Ein Vergleich* (Munich: Oldenbourg, 2010), 101.

11. Karl Felix Wolff, *Rassenlehre. Neue Gedanken zur Anthropologie, Politik, Wirtschaft, Volkspflege und Ethik* (Leipzig: Kapitzsch, 1927), 171, and 173 for the widespread currency of this view in Europe. Wolff, it should be said, nevertheless believed that race mixing doomed America to decline. For the place of America in European perceptions of the international scene, see generally Adam Tooze, *The Deluge: The Great War, America and the Remaking of the Global Order, 1916–1931* (New York: Penguin, 2014).

12. E.g., Wahrhold Drascher, *Die Vorherrschaft der Weissen Rasse* (Stuttgart: Deutsche Verlags-Anstalt, 1936), 340; and the treatment in Michael Kater, *Different Drummers: Jazz in the Culture of Nazi Germany* (Oxford: Oxford University Press, 1992),

29–56. For German interest in American Fordism and industrial society, see Mary Nolan, *Visions of Modernity: American Business and the Modernization of Germany* (New York: Oxford University Press, 1994); Volker Berghahn, *Industriegesellschaft und Kulturtransfer: Die deutsch-amerikanischen Beziehungen im 20. Jahrhundert* (Göttingen: Vandenhoeck & Ruprecht, 2010), e.g., 28–29.

13. Hitler, *Mein Kampf*, 143–44 ed. (Munich: Eher, 1935), 479 (= Hitler, *Mein Kampf. Eine kritische Edition*, ed. Christian Hartmann, Thomas Vordermayer, Othmar Plöckinger, and Roman Töppel [Munich: Institut für Zeitgeschichte, 2016], 2:1093–95).

14. See Victoria de Grazia, *Irresistible Empire: America's Advance through Twentieth-Century Europe* (Cambridge, MA: Harvard University Press, 2005); Egbert Klautke, *Unbegrenzte Möglichkeiten. "Amerikanisierung" in Deutschland und Frankreich (1900–1933)* (Wiesbaden: Steiner, 2003).

15. These quotes are from the Nazi Party newspaper *Völkischer Beobachter*, reproduced in Hans-Jürgen Schröder, *Deutschland und die Vereinigten Staaten 1933–1939; Wirtschaft und Politik in der Entwicklung des deutschamerikanischen Gegensatzes* (Wiesbaden: Steiner, 1970), 93, and generally 93–119. Detlef Junker sees the turning point as coming with the Quarantine Speech in October 1937. Junker, "Hitler's Perception of Franklin D. Roosevelt and the United States of America," in *FDR and His Contemporaries: Foreign Perceptions of an American President*, ed. Cornelius A. van Minnen and John F. Sears (New York: St. Martin's, 1992), 143–56, 150–51. See also Klaus P. Fischer, *Hitler and America* (Philadelphia: University of Pennsylvania Press, 2011), 65–69. For further discussion, see below, Chapter 1, text at Note 28.

16. Schröder, *Deutschland und die Vereinigten Staaten*, 93–119; and for "the fascist New Deal," James Q. Whitman, "Commercial Law and the American Volk: A Note on Llewellyn's German Sources for the Uniform Commercial Code," *Yale Law Journal* 97 (1987): 156–75, 170. European progressives too were interested in the New Deal, of course: see Daniel Rodgers, *Atlantic Crossings: Social Politics in a Progressive Age* (Cambridge, MA: Harvard University Press, 1998), 410–11.

17. Detlef Junker, "The Continuity of Ambivalence," in *Transatlantic Images and Perceptions: Germany and America since 1776*, ed. David E. Barclay and Elisabeth Glaser-Schmidt (New York: Cambridge University Press, 1997), 246.

18. Wulf Siewert, "Amerika am Wendepunkt," *Wille und Macht*, April 15, 1935, 22.

19. While Junker, "Hitler's Perception of Franklin D. Roosevelt," points to the Quarantine Speech of 1937, Steven Casey, *Cautious Crusade: Franklin D. Roosevelt, American Public Opinion, and the War against Nazi Germany* (New York: Oxford University Press, 2001), 40, documents the reluctance of FDR to name Hitler until 1939. See also ibid., 9. Philipp Gassert by contrast points, somewhat tentatively, to the State of the Union speech in January 1936. Gassert, " 'Without Concessions to Marxist or Communist Thought': Fordism in Germany, 1923–1939," in Barclay and Glaser-Schmidt, *Transatlantic Images and Perceptions*, 238.

20. Ira Katznelson, *Fear Itself: The New Deal and the Origins of Our Time* (New York: Liveright, 2013).

21. For a call for friendship on the basis of shared racism, see Waldemar Hartmann, "Deutschland und die USA. Wege zu gegenseitigem Verstehen," *Nationalsozialistische Monatshefte* 4 (November 1933): 493–94.

22. Katznelson, *Fear Itself*, 126–27. It is also important to observe that adulation of the American president could be found elsewhere in Europe as well. See David Ellwood, *The Shock of America: Europe and the Challenge of the Century* (New York: Oxford University Press, 2012), 186–93.

23. For studies on the resemblances and influences, see John Garraty, "The New Deal, National Socialism, and the Great Depression," *American Historical Review* 78 (1973): 907–44; Wolfgang Schivelbusch, *Three New Deals: Reflections on Roosevelt's America, Mussolini's Italy, and Hitler's Germany, 1933–1939*, trans. Jefferson Chase (New York: Metropolitan, 2006); and for Italy, see James Q. Whitman, "Of Corporatism, Fascism and the First New Deal," *American Journal of Comparative Law* 39 (1991): 747–78.

24. Grill and Jenkins, "Nazis and the American South."

25. For this program, conducted under the cover of war, and its background in German legal thought, see Christian Merkel, *"Tod den Idioten"—Eugenik und Euthanasie in juristischer Rezeption vom Kaiserreich zur Hitlerzeit* (Berlin: Logos, 2006), 20–21 and passim.

26. Stefan Kühl, *The Nazi Connection: Eugenics, American Racism, and German National Socialism* (New York: Oxford University Press, 1994), 37 and passim.

27. E.g., Randall Hansen and Desmond King, "Eugenic Ideas, Political Interest and Policy Variance: Immigration and Sterilization Policy in Britain and the U.S.," *World Politics* 53, no. 2 (2001): 237–63; Véronique Mottier, "Eugenics and the State: Policy-Making in Comparative Perspective," in *Oxford Handbook of the History of Eugenics*, ed. Alison Bashford and Philippa Levine (New York: Oxford University Press, 2010), 135.

28. Timothy Snyder, *Black Earth: The Holocaust as History and Warning* (New York: Tim Duggan Books, 2015), 12.

29. Ibid.

30. Quoted partially and discussed in Ian Kershaw, *Fateful Choices: Ten Decisions That Changed the World* (New York: Penguin, 2007), 386–87; cf. Carroll P. Kakel, *The American West and the Nazi East: A Comparative and Interpretive Perspective* (New York: Palgrave Macmillan, 2011), 1. I have added a fuller and slightly altered translation of the passage quoted by Kershaw, from Adolf Hitler, *Reden, Schriften, Anordnungen* (1928; Munich: Saur, 1994), 3:1, p. 161.

31. For a survey of the literature, see Kakel, *American West and the Nazi East*, 1–2. See also David Blackbourn, "The Conquest of Nature and the Mystique of the Eastern Frontier in Germany," in *Germans, Poland, and Colonial Expansion in the East*, ed. Robert Nelson (New York: Palgrave Macmillan, 2009), 152–53; Alan Steinweis, "Eastern Europe and the Notion of the 'Frontier' in Germany to 1945," *Yearbook of European Studies* 13 (1999): 56–70; Philipp Gassert, *Amerika im Dritten Reich: Ideologie, Propaganda und Volksmeinung, 1933–1945* (Stuttgart: Steiner, 1997), 95–97.

32. Guettel, *German Expansionism*, 193–95 and 209–11, makes unpersuasive efforts to dismiss this literature, essentially by denying the force of examples, no matter how many are given.

33. Norman Rich, "Hitler's Foreign Policy," in *The Origins of the Second World War Reconsidered: The A.J.P. Taylor Debate after Twenty-Five Years*, ed. Gordon Martel (Boston: Allen & Unwin, 1986), 136.

34. See Chapter 2 for the *Preußische Denkschrift* of 1933 and other texts and discussions.

35. Gustav Klemens Schmelzeisen, *Das Recht im Nationalsozialistischen Weltbild. Grundzüge des deutschen Rechts*, 3rd ed. (Leipzig: Kohlhammer, 1936), 84.

36. See Chapter 2.

37. Quoted in Bernstein, "Jim Crow and Nuremberg Laws."

38. See, e.g., the remarks of David Dyzenhaus, *Legality and Legitimacy: Carl Schmitt, Hans Kelsen and Hermann Heller in Weimar* (Oxford: Oxford University Press, 1997), 100.

39. On Pound, see Stephen H. Norwood, *The Third Reich in the Ivory Tower* (Cambridge and New York: Cambridge University Press, 2009), 56–57; and on American Nazism more broadly, see Sander A. Diamond, *The Nazi Movement in the United States, 1924–1941* (Ithaca, NY: Cornell University Press, 1974).

40. Veering in that direction: Hermann Ploppa, *Hitlers Amerikanische Lehrer: Die Eliten der USA als Geburtshelfer der Nazi-Bewegung* (Sterup: Liepsen, 2008).

CHAPTER 1: MAKING NAZI FLAGS AND NAZI CITIZENS

1. Hitler, *Mein Kampf*, 143–44 ed. (Munich: Eher, 1935), 313–14. For the earlier version, see Hitler, *Mein Kampf. Eine kritische Edition*, ed. Christian Hartmann, Thomas Vordermayer, Othmar Plöckinger, and Roman Töppel (Munich: Institut für Zeitgeschichte, 2016), 1:743, and the discussion in Note 35.

2. "Reich Adopts Swastika as Nation's Official Flag; Hitler's Reply to 'Insult,'" *New York Times*, September 16, 1935, A1.

3. E.g., Wilhelm Stuckart, "Nationalsozialismus und Staatsrecht," in *Grundlagen, Aufbau und Wirtschaftsordnung des nationalsozialistischen Staates*, ed. H.-H. Lammers et al. (Berlin: Spaeth & Linde, 1936), 15:23; *Meyers Lexikon*, 8th ed. (Leipzig: Bibliographisches Institut, 1940), 8:525, s.v. "Nürnberger Gesetze."

4. Jay Meader, "Heat Wave Disturbing Peace, July 1935 Chapter 111," *New York Daily News*, June 13, 2000, http://www.nydailynews.com/archives/news/heat-wave -disturbing-peace-july-1935-chapter-111-article-1.874082. For the larger history, see Klaus P. Fischer, *Hitler and America* (Philadelphia: University of Pennsylvania Press, 2011), 50–52; Thomas Kessner, *Fiorello H. La Guardia and the Making of Modern New York* (New York: McGraw-Hill, 1989), 401–2.

5. See "Text of Police Department's Report on the Bremen Riot," *New York Times*, August 2, 1935. For the *Bremen* and its sister ship the *Europa*, see Arnold Kludas,

Record Breakers of the North Atlantic: Blue Riband Liners, 1838–1952 (London: Chatham, 2000), 109–17.

6. *U.S. Department of State. Press Releases* (1935), 101.

7. See, e.g., Fischer, *Hitler and America*, 49.

8. "Louis B. Brodsky, 86, Former Magistrate," *New York Times*, May 1, 1970, 35. For the correct date of his degree, "New York University Commencement," *New York Times*, June 7, 1901, 9.

9. Detlef Sahm, *Die Vereinigten Staaten von Amerika und das Problem der nationalen Einheit* (Berlin: Buchholz & Weisswange, 1936), 92–96.

10. For his appointment first by Mayor John F. Hylan and then by Mayor Jimmy Walker, see "Louis B. Brodsky, 86, Former Magistrate," *New York Times*, May 1, 1970, 35.

11. New York Inferior Criminal Courts Act, Title V, §§ 70, 70a, *Code of Criminal Procedure of the State of New York*, 20th ed. (1920).

12. See Herbert Mitgang, *The Man Who Rode the Tiger: The Life and Times of Judge Samuel Seabury* (New York: Lippincott, 1963), 190–91. It seems that Brodsky had made quite a fortune in market speculation.

13. See Terry Golway, *Machine Made: Tammany Hall and the Creation of Modern American Politics* (New York: Liveright, 2014), e.g., 253–54.

14. Jay Gertzman, *Bookleggers and Smuthounds: The Trade in Erotica, 1920–1940* (Philadelphia: University of Pennsylvania Press, 1999), 167.

15. "Court Upholds Nudity. No Longer Considered Indecent in Nightclubs, Magistrate Says," *New York Times*, April 7, 1935, F17.

16. Ibid.

17. "Brodsky Releases 5 in Bremen Riot," *New York Times*, September 7, 1935, 1, 5.

18. E.g., "U.S. Apology for Reich. Hull Expresses Regrets on Brodsky Remarks," *Montreal Gazette*, September 16, 1935. See generally the documents in *Foreign Relations of the United States* (1935), 2:485–90.

19. See, e.g., Ian Kershaw, *Hitler, 1889–1936: Hubris* (New York: Norton, 1999), 419–68.

20. Erlaß des Reichspräsidenten über die vorläufige Regelung der Flaggenhissung (vom 12, März 1933), Reichsgesetzblatt (1933), 1:103.

21. I follow here the analysis of Dirk Blasius, *Carl Schmitt: Preussischer Staatsrat in Hitlers Reich* (Göttingen: Vandenhoeck & Ruprecht, 2001), 109.

22. Goebbels, entry for September 9, 1935, in *Tagebücher*, ed. Angela Hermann, Hartmut Mehringer, Anne Munding, and Jana Richter (Munich: Institut für Zeitgeschichte, 2005), 3/1. Discussed in Peter Longerich, *Politik der Vernichtung. Eine Gesamtdarstellung der nationalsozialistischen Judenverfolgung* (Munich: Piper, 1998), 622n198.

23. Johannes Stoye, *USA. Lernt Um! Sinn und Bedeutung der Roosevelt Revolution* (Leipzig: W. Goldmann, 1935), 140.

24. See, e.g., Arthur Holitscher, *Wiedersehen mit Amerika* (Berlin: Fischer, 1930), 45–49.

25. "Thoroughly decent and honorable" is my translation of "in loyalster Weise." Max Domarus, *Hitler: Reden und Proklamationen, 1932–1945* (Neustadt a.d. Aisch, 1962), 1:537.

26. Hitler, in ibid., 1:536–37.

27. Ibid., 1:538: "wir bedauern das amerikanische Volk darum, daß es gezwungen war, einer solchen Verunglimpfung zuzusehen." For the "frecher Jude" Brodsky, see ibid.

28. Philipp Gassert, " 'Without Concessions to Marxist or Communist Thought': Fordism in Germany, 1923–1939," in *Transatlantic Images and Perceptions: Germany and America since 1776*, ed. David E. Barclay and Elisabeth Glaser-Schmidt (New York: Cambridge University Press, 1997), 239. For 1937 as the year of the turning point, see Junker, "Hitler's Perception of Franklin D. Roosevelt," 150–51; Fischer, *Hitler and America*, 65–69.

29. Albrecht Wirth, *Völkische Weltgeschichte (1879–1933)* (Braunschweig: Westermann, 1934), 10. Wirth spoke of "Westarier," but for the sake of simplicity I have given the translation "Aryan." This passage already appeared in the 1924 edition of Wirth's book, though at the time with a frontispiece of a bust of Hindenburg. Wirth, *Völkische Weltgeschichte*, 5th ed. (Braunschweig/Hamburg: Westermann, 1924), 10.

30. Thurgood Marshall, "Reflections on the Bicentennial of the United States Constitution," *Harvard Law Review* 101 (1987): 2.

31. Wahrhold Drascher, *Die Vorherrschaft der Weissen Rasse* (Stuttgart: Deutsche Verlags-Anstalt, 1936), 159–60. For Drascher and his "vielbeachtetes, von der Partei jedoch nicht einhellig gutgeheißenes Buch," see Albrecht Hagemann, *Südafrika und das "Dritte Reich"* (Frankfurt: Campus, 1989), 117–18.

32. Drascher, *Vorherrschaft der Weissen Rasse*, 339.

33. Ibid., 217.

34. Alfred Rosenberg, "Die rassische Bedingtheit der Aussenpolitik," *Hochschule und Ausland*, October 1933, 8–9.

35. Hitler, *Mein Kampf*, 313–14. Until 1930 the passage read "bis auch er der Blutschande zum Opfer fällt," rather than "solange nicht auch er der Blutschande zum Opfer fällt." Apparently Hitler became more willing to consider the possibility that America would survive as a race state in the interim. See Hitler, *Mein Kampf. Eine kritische Edition*, 1:743.

36. For example, Drascher believed that the United States had proved its fidelity to the white cause, but that it might withdraw behind its borders and so cease to contribute to the global fight for white supremacy. See Drascher, *Vorherrschaft der Weissen Rasse*, 294–95; and for the uncertainty about whether the United States would remain faithful to the racist cause, see ibid., 351.

37. Waldemar Hartmann, "Deutschland und die USA. Wege zu gegenseitigem Verstehen," *Nationalsozialistische Monatshefte* 4 (November 1933): 481–94; Hartmann, "Politische Probleme der U.S.A.," *Nationalsozialistische Monatshefte* 4 (November 1933): 494–506; Karl Bömer, "Das neue Deutschland in der amerikanischen Presse," *Nationalsozialistische Monatshefte* 4 (November 1933): 506–9.

38. Reichsgesetzblatt (1935), 1:1146, https://de.wikisource.org/wiki/Reichsb%C3%BCrgergesetz.

39. Domarus, *Hitler*, 1:538.

40. For the sake of simplicity, I have translated *Zuchthaus* as "hard labor." For a fuller account of what *Zuchthaus* was, see James Q. Whitman, *Harsh Justice: Criminal*

Punishment and the Widening Divide between America and Europe (New York: Oxford University Press, 2003), 132.

41. Reichsgesetzblatt (1935), 1:1146, https://de.wikisource.org/wiki/Gesetz_zum_Schutze_des_deutschen_Blutes_und_der_deutschen_Ehre.

42. "Nazis Bar Jews as Citizens; Make Swastika Sole Flag in Reply to Insult," *New York Herald Tribune*, September 16, 1935, 1.

43. For an account looking beyond the conventional focus on segregation, see Ariela J. Gross, *What Blood Won't Tell: A History of Race on Trial in America* (Cambridge, MA: Harvard University Press, 2008), 5–7.

44. 347 US 483 (1954).

45. 163 US 537 (1896).

46. See the Introduction.

47. E.g., James E. Falkowski, *Indian Law/Race Law: A Five-Hundred Year History* (New York: Praeger, 1992), 47–80.

48. Ian Haney López, *White by Law* (New York: New York University Press, 2006), 27–28.

49. E.g., Christopher Waldrep, "Substituting Law for the Lash: Emancipation and Legal Formalism in a Mississippi County Court," *Journal of American History* 82 (1996): 1425–51, 1426; Bruce Ackerman and Jennifer Nou, "Canonizing the Civil Rights Revolution: The People and the Poll Tax," *Northwestern Law Review* 103 (2009): 63–148.

50. See below, "American Second-Class Citizenship."

51. Peggy Pascoe, *What Comes Naturally: Miscegenation Law and the Making of Race in America* (Oxford: Oxford University Press, 2009).

52. 388 US 1 (1967).

53. Haney López, *White by Law*, 27–34.

54. Immigration and Nationality Act of 1965 (Pub. L. 89-236, 79 Stat. 911, enacted June 30, 1968). For the limits to its liberalization, see Christian Joppke, *Selecting by Origin: Ethnic Migration in the Liberal State* (Cambridge, MA: Harvard University Press, 2005), 57–59.

55. Stefan Kühl, *The Nazi Connection: Eugenics, American Racism, and German National Socialism* (New York: Oxford University Press, 1994), 21–22, 38–39.

56. An Act to Establish an Uniform Rule of Naturalization, ch. 3, 1 Stat. 103 (1790). For the historic importance of the 1790 act, see David Scott Fitzgerald and David Cook-Martin, *Culling the Masses: The Democratic Origins of Racist Immigration Policy in the Americas* (Cambridge, MA: Harvard University Press, 2014), 82; for its place in the larger history of race-based immigration and naturalization law, see Haney López, *White by Law*, 31; and for its "uncontroversial" character at the time of passage, see Rogers Smith, *Civic Ideals: Conflicting Visions of Citizenship in U.S. History* (New Haven, CT: Yale University Press, 1997), 159–60; Douglas Bradburn, *The Citizenship Revolution: Politics and the Creation of the American Union, 1774–1804* (Charlottesville: University of Virginia Press, 2009), 260.

57. This was Heinrich Krieger, *Das Rassenrecht in den Vereinigten Staaten* (Berlin: Junker & Dünnhaupt, 1936), 74. For the absence of any French ban, see Peter

Sahlins, *Unnaturally French: Foreign Citizens in the Old Regime and After* (Ithaca, NY: Cornell University Press, 2004), 183–84. I note however that a decree of August 9, 1777 forbade the entry of "noirs, mulâtres et gens de couleur" into France, with an exception for personal servants. Joseph-Nicolas Guyot, *Repertoire Universel et Raisonné de Jurisprudence* (Paris: Panckoucke, 1778), 23:383–86. For the contrasting atmosphere during the French Revolution, see Robert Forster, "Who is a Citizen?," *French Politics and Society* 7 (1989): 50–64, and for the contrast with the larger Atlantic world see Alan Taylor, *American Revolutions: A Continental History, 1750–1804* (New York: Norton, 2016), 21–23.

58. Otto Koellreutter, *Grundriß der allgemeinen Staatslehre* (Tübingen: Mohr, 1933), 51.

59. See Gerald L. Neuman, "The Lost Century of American Immigration Law (1776–1875)," *Columbia Law Review* 93 (1993): 1866–67.

60. Tyler Anbinder, *Nativism and Slavery: The Northern Know Nothings and the Politics of the 1850's* (New York: Oxford University Press, 1992), 136.

61. See Philip P. Choy, Marlon K. Hom, and Lorraine Dong, eds., *The Coming Man: 19th Century American Perceptions of the Chinese* (Seattle: University of Washington Press, 1994), 123; M. Margaret McKeown and Emily Ryo, "The Lost Sanctuary: Examining Sex Trafficking through the Lens of United States v. Ah Sou," *Cornell International Law Journal* 41 (2008): 746; Ernesto Hernández-López, "Global Migrations and Imagined Citizenship: Examples from Slavery, Chinese Exclusion, and When Questioning Birthright Citizenship," *Texas Wesleyan Law Review* 14 (2008): 268.

62. See Andrew Gyory, *Closing the Gate: Race, Politics, and the Chinese Exclusion Act* (Chapel Hill: University of North Carolina Press, 1998), 1.

63. See Cal. Const. of 1879, art. XIX, § 4 (repealed 1952); see also Iris Chang, *The Chinese in America* (New York: Viking, 2003), 43–45, 75, 119–20, 176.

64. Chinese Exclusion Act of 1882, ch. 126, 22 Stat. 58, repealed by Chinese Exclusion Repeal Act of 1943, ch. 344, § 1, 57 Stat. 600; see also *Chae Chan Ping v. United States*, 130 US 581 (1889) (The Chinese Exclusion Case) (upholding the Chinese Exclusion Act of 1888, ch. 1015, 25 Stat. 476).

65. Sucheng Chan, *Entry Denied: Exclusion and the Chinese Community in America, 1882–1943* (Philadelphia: Temple University Press, 1991), vii–viii; Terri Yuh-lin Chen, "Hate Violence as Border Patrol: An Asian American Theory of Hate Violence," *Asian American Law Journal* 7 (2000): 69–101; see also Ronald T. Takaki, *Strangers from a Different Shore: A History of Asian Americans* (Boston: Little, Brown, 1989), 203.

66. An Act to Amend the Immigration Laws of the United States, H.R. 7864, 54th Cong. (1896).

67. Grover Cleveland, Message from the President of the United States, Returning to the House of Representatives, without his approval House Bill numbered 7864, entitled "An Act to Amend the Immigration Laws of the United States," S. Doc. No. 54-185, at 1–4 (2d sess. 1897).

68. An Act to Regulate the Immigration of Aliens to, and the Residence of Aliens in, the United States ("Asiatic Barred Zone Act"), H.R. 10384, Pub. L. 301, 39 Stat. 874., 64th Cong. (1917).

69. An Act to Limit the Immigration of Aliens into the United States ("Emergency Quota Act"), H.R. 4075, 77th Cong. ch. 8 (1921).

70. An Act to Limit the Immigration of Aliens into the United States, and for Other Purposes ("The 1924 Immigration Act"), H.R. 7995; Pub. L. 68-139; 43 Stat. 153., 68th Cong. (1924).

71. Mae Ngai, "The Architecture of Race in American Immigration Law: A Reexamination of the Immigration Act of 1924," *Journal of American History* 86 (1999): 69. In an important article, Son Thierry Ly and Patrick Weil show the 1921 statute was in fact designed to curb racist policies as much as possible. Ly and Weil, "The Anti-Racist Origin of the Quota System," *Social Research* 77 (2010): 45–78. What matters for my purposes here, however, is that the 1921 statute remained race-based, and that the Nazis perceived it as a racist measure.

72. John William Burgess, *Political Science and Comparative Constitutional Law* (London: Ginn & Co., 1890), 1:42, quoted and discussed in the Marilyn Lake and Henry Reynolds, *Drawing the Global Colour Line: White Men's Countries and the International Challenge of Racial Equality* (Cambridge: Cambridge University Press, 2008), 139. See generally ibid., and Aziz Rana, *The Two Faces of American Freedom* (Cambridge, MA: Harvard University Press, 2010), 3 and often.

73. Lake and Reynolds, *Drawing the Global Colour Line*, 164, 315–20.

74. Ibid., 17–45 (speaking of course of the colony of Victoria at the time); Charles A. Price, *The Great White Walls Are Built: Restrictive Immigration to North America and Australasia, 1836–1888* (Canberra: Australian National University Press, 1974).

75. Lake and Reynolds, *Drawing the Global Colour Line*, 71–72, 119–25.

76. Quoted in Joppke, *Selecting by Origin*, 34, and generally on the United States and Australia, 31–49.

77. Fitzgerald and Cook-Martin, *Culling the Masses*, 7.

78. André Siegfried, *Die Vereinigten Staaten von Amerika: Volk, Wirtschaft, Politik*, 2nd ed., trans. C. & M. Loosli-Usteri (Leipzig: Orell Füssli, 1928), 79–108 and 100 for the character of American immigration legislation. The French original was published in 1927.

79. E.g., Jean Pluyette, *La Sélection de l'immigration en France et la doctrine des races* (Paris: Bossuet, 1930), 58–69; M. Valet, *Les Restrictions à l'Immigration* (Paris: Sirey, 1930), 23–24.

80. Lake and Reynolds, *Drawing the Global Colour Line*, 29, 35, 49–74 (influence of Bryce), 80, 119, 129–31, 138–44, 225, 269.

81. See, e.g., Pierre Wurtz, *La Question de l'Immigration aux États-Unis. Son État Actuel* (Paris: Dreux and Schneider, 1925), 259–60.

82. Theodor Fritsch, *Handbuch der Judenfrage*, 26th ed. (Hamburg: Hanseatische Druck- und Verlagsantstalt, 1907), 8–9.

83. Mark Mazower, *Hitler's Empire: How the Nazis Ruled Europe* (New York: Penguin, 2008), 584.

84. For native Americans, see Burt Estes Howard, *Das Amerikanische Bürgerrecht* (Leipzig: Duncker & Humblot, 1904), 35–38; for Puerto Ricans, see Paul Darmstädter, *Die Vereinigten Staaten von Amerika. Ihre politische, wirtschaftliche und soziale Entwicklung* (Leipzig: Quelle & Meyer, 1909), 208.

85. *Dred Scott v. Sandford*, 60 US (19 How.) 393 (1857), superseded by constitutional amendment, US Const. Amend. XIV.

86. Stephen Breyer, "Making Our Democracy Work: The Yale Lectures," *Yale Law Journal* 120 (2011): 2012–13 ("Most historians would agree today that, if Dred Scott had any effect on the Civil War, it tended to cause that war, not to prevent it"). But see Jack M. Balkin and Sanford Levinson, "Thirteen Ways of Looking at Dred Scott," *Chicago-Kent Law Review* 82 (2007): 67 ("Today many people believe that Dred Scott hastened the Civil War, although . . . this is by no means clear—it may actually have delayed it by several years").

87. US Const. Amends. XIV, XV.

88. In the 1850s, Connecticut and Massachusetts amended their constitutions to include literacy requirements for voting and holding political office. Conn. Const. of 1818, Art. XI (1855); Alexander Keyssar, *The Right to Vote: The Contested History of Democracy in the United States* (New York: Basic Books, 2000), 144–45.

89. Lake and Reynolds, *Drawing the Global Colour Line*, 63.

90. It was not until 1915 that the Court struck down the grandfather clauses, which exempted from literacy requirements illiterate white voters, but not black voters who had no basis for being grandfathered in. *Guinn v. United States*, 238 US 347 (1915).

91. See, e.g., Daryl Levinson and Benjamin I. Sachs, "Political Entrenchment and Public Law," *Yale Law Journal* 125 (2015): 414.

92. See, e.g., *Breedlove v. Suttles*, 302 US 277, 283 (1937), overruled by *Harper v. Virginia State Bd. of Elections*, 383 US 663 (1966); *Lassiter v. Northampton Cty. Bd. of Elections*, 360 US 45, 53–54 (1959).

93. Max Weber, "Die Protestantischen Sekten und der Geist des Kapitalismus," reprinted in *Gesammelte Aufsätze zur Religionssoziologie*, 2nd ed. (Tübingen: Mohr, 1922), 1:207–36, 1:217.

94. Ibid.

95. Eduard Meyer, *Die Vereinigten Staaten von Amerika. Geschichte, Kultur, Verfassung und Politik* (Frankfurt: Keller, 1920), 93; cf., e.g., Otto Hoetzsch, *Die Vereinigten Staaten von Nordamerika* (Bielefeld/Leipzig: Velhagen & Kalsing, 1904), 174.

96. Robert Michels, *Wirtschaftliche und politische Betrachtungen zur alten und neuen Welt* (Leipzig: Gloeckner, 1928), 10, and generally 10–12, 29–30.

97. Konrad Haebler et al., *Weltgeschichte* (Leipzig: Bibliographisches Institut, 1922), 250.

98. Darmstädter, *Die Vereinigten Staaten von Amerika*, 216.

99. *Der Grosse Brockhaus. Handbuch des Wissens*, 15th ed. (Leipzig: Brockhaus, 1932), 13:253, s.v. "Negerfrage"; and, e.g., Rudolf Hensel, *Die Neue Welt. Ein Amerikabuch* (Hellerau: Hegner, 1929), 106–7.

100. For an account from the early 1930s, see Dudley McGovney, "Our Noncitizen Nationals, Who Are They?," *California Law Review* 22 (1934): 593–635.

101. See now Gerald Neuman and Tomiko Brown-Nagin, eds., *Reconsidering the Insular Cases: The Past and Future of the American Empire* (Cambridge, MA: Harvard University Press, 2015).

102. See David Ellwood, *The Shock of America: Europe and the Challenge of the Century* (New York: Oxford University Press, 2012), 22–25.

103. E.g., Darmstädter, *Die Vereinigten Staaten von Amerika*, 208.

104. Quoted in Frank Degenhardt, *Zwischen Machtstaat und Völkerbund. Erich Kaufmann (1880–1972)* (Baden-Baden: Nomos, 2008), 1; see further ibid., 124–26 for his biography, including his associations with Moeller van den Bruck and the Juniklub. For his relationship with Carl Schmitt, see Stefan Hanke, "Carl Schmitt und Erich Kaufmann—Gemeines in Bonn und Berlin," in *Die Juristen der Universität Bonn im "Dritten Reich,"* ed. Mathias Schmoeckel (Cologne: Böhlau, 2004), 388–407; and for an assessment of his philosophy of the state, see Daniel Kachel, "Das Wesen des Staates—Kaufmanns frühe Rechtsphilosophie," in Schmoeckel, *Die Juristen*, 408–24.

105. Another fascinating example is of course Ernst Kantorowicz, with his mystical rightist views of the Reich. For an account of his career, which brought him "precariously close to the Nazis," and the complexities of placing him politically, see Conrad Leyser, "Introduction" to Ernst Kantorowicz, *The King's Two Bodies: A Study in Medieval Political Theology*, new ed., ed. William Chester Jordan (Princeton: Princeton University Press, 2016), ix–xxiii, xiii, and generally xi–xv.

106. Erich Kaufmann, *Auswärtige Gewalt und Koloniale Gewalt in den Vereinigten Staaten von Amerika* (Leipzig: Duncker & Humblot, 1908), 139.

107. Ibid., 156.

108. See esp. Gnaeus Flavius [Hermann Kantorowicz], *Der Kampf um die Rechtswissenschaft* (Heidelberg: Winter, 1906), 7–8. This is not the place to investigate the crosscurrents of influence by which the German Free School built theories on the basis of an idealization of the common law that then influenced American legal thinkers.

109. Kaufmann, *Auswärtige Gewalt*, 11. Of course, Kaufmann's book would not have been a permissible citation during the Nazi period, so it is impossible to say whether it influenced Nazi perceptions of the United States.

110. Hugo Münsterberg, *Die Amerikaner* (Berlin: Mittler, 1912), 1:208–9.

111. Ernst Freund, *Das öffentliche Recht der Vereinigten Staaten von Amerika* (Tübingen: Mohr, 1911), 62.

112. Ibid., 63–64. It is worth observing that similar views would be expressed in the Fourth Communist International in 1922. See *Resolutions and Theses of the Fourth Congress of the Communist International, Held in Moscow, Nov. 7 to Dec. 3, 1922* (London: Communist International, n.d.), 85–86. A fuller account of the place of this aspect of American law on the international scene would have to treat communist engagement as well. In the interests of brevity, I leave that topic aside, though.

113. Wm. Weber, "Die auswärtige Politik der Vereinigten Staaten," *Preussische Jahrbücher* 145 (1911): 345–54, 346. Weber was a Pennsylvania pastor.

114. Nationalsozialistisches Parteiprogramm (1920), http://www.documentarchiv.de/wr/1920/nsdap-programm.html.

115. Jürgen Peter Schmidt, "Hitlers Amerikabild," *Geschichte in Wissenschaft und Unterricht* 53 (2002): 714–26; cf. Inge Marszolek, "Das Amerikabild im Dritten Reich," in *Amerika und Europa. Mars und Venus? Das Bild Amerikas in Europa*, ed. Rudolf von Thadden and Alexander Escudier (Göttingen: Wallstein, 2004), 49–64.

116. Hitler, *Mein Kampf*, 488–90 (= Hitler, *Mein Kampf. Eine kritische Edition*, 2:1115–17).

117. Kühl rightly highlights this passage, but American legal scholars seem to have missed it. Kühl, *Nazi Connection*, 26.

118. Hitler, "Außenpolitische Standortbestimmung nach der Reichstagswahl, Juni–Juli 1928," in Hitler, *Reden, Schriften, Anordnungen* (1928; Munich: Saur, 1994), 2A:92.

119. Gerhard Weinberg, *Hitlers Zweites Buch. Ein Dokument aus dem Jahr 1928* (Stuttgart: Deutsche Verlags-Anstalt, 1961), 130 and 132.

120. Alexander Graf Brockdorff, *Amerikanische Weltherrschaft?*, 2nd ed. (Berlin: Albrecht, 1930), 29; cf., e.g., Karl Felix Wolff, *Rassenlehre. Neue Gedanken zur Anthropologie, Politik, Wirtschaft, Volkspflege und Ethik* (Leipzig: Kapitzsch, 1927), 173.

121. His views were not to darken until the outbreak of World War II. See Fischer, *Hitler and America*, 10.

122. Weinberg, *Hitlers Zweites Buch*, 132. For other related statements, see ibid., 121, 125.

123. Ibid., 132.

124. Quoted partially and discussed in Ian Kershaw, *Fateful Choices: Ten Decisions That Changed the World* (New York: Penguin, 2007), 386–87; for the original, see Hitler, *Reden, Schriften, Anordnungen*, 3:1, p. 161.

125. Detlef Junker, "Die Kontinuität der Ambivalenz: Deutsche Bilder von Amerika, 1933–1945," in *Gesellschaft und Diplomatie im transatlantischen Kontext*, ed. Michael Wala (Stuttgart: Steiner, 1999), 171–72, quoted passage at 171.

126. Philipp Gassert, *Amerika im Dritten Reich: Ideologie, Propaganda und Volksmeinung, 1933–1945* (Stuttgart: Steiner, 1997), 95–97, quoted language at 96.

127. Ibid.

128. E.g., Hans Reimer, *Rechtsschutz der Rasse im neuen Staat* (Greifswald: Adler, 1934), 47.

129. Junker argues that the Nazis took a generally benign view of the United States in the early 1930s. Junker, "Kontinuität," 166–67. From the point of view of the legal history traced in this book, it must be said that the Nazi view of the United States was perhaps more complex than Junker's judgment allows.

130. Hartmann, "Deutschland und die USA," 493–94. Hartmann was calling for cultural exchanges, but in the larger context of broader hopes for understanding.

131. Juliane Wetzel, "Auswanderung aus Deutschland," in *Die Juden in Deutschland 1933–1945*, ed. Wolfgang Benz (Munich: Beck, 1988), 414; Philippe Burrin, *Hitler et les Juifs. Genèse d'un génocide* (Paris: Éditions du Seuil, 1989), 37–65.

132. Wetzel, "Auswanderung," 426.

133. Hans Christian Jasch, *Staatssekretär Wilhelm Stuckart und die Judenpolitik* (Munich: Oldenbourg, 2012), 316–40 (Wannsee), 392–424 (war crimes trial).

134. Stuckart, "Nationalsozialismus und Staatsrecht," 15:23. The version of this passage in the introduction to Wilhelm Stuckart and Hans Globke, *Kommentare zur deutschen Rassengesetzgebung* (Berlin: Beck, 1936), 1:15, was more restrained. For a detailed account of Stuckart's shift from the politics of expulsion to the politics of annihilation, see Jasch, *Staatssekretär Wilhelm Stuckart*, 290–372.

135. Reichsgesetzblatt (1933), 1:529.

136. Uwe Dietrich Adam, *Judenpolitik im Dritten Reich* (Düsseldorf: Droste, 1972), 80–81.

137. Ibid.

138. Jörg Schmidt, *Otto Koellreutter, 1883–1972* (New York: Lang, 1995); Michael Stolleis, "Koellreutter, Otto," in *Neue Deutsche Biographie*, vol. 12 (1979), 324–25, https://www.deutsche-biographie.de/gnd119235935.html#ndbcontent. For Koellreutter's role in Munich and Nazi Germany, see also Michael Stolleis, *A History of Public Law in Germany, 1914–1945*, trans. Thomas Dunlap (Oxford: Oxford University Press, 2004), 300 and, e.g., 327. Much later on, Koellreutter became disaffected with the regime.

139. Rolf Peter, "Bevölkerungspolitik, Erb- und Rassenpflege in der Gesetzgebung des Dritten Reiches," *Deutsches Recht* 7 (1937): 238n1; for other British Empire laws, see above, text at Notes 73–78.

140. Koellreutter, *Grundriß der allgemeinen Staatslehre*, 51–52.

141. See, e.g., Berthold Schenk Graf von Stauffenberg, "Die Entstehung der Staatsangehörigkeit und das Völkerrecht," *Zeitschrift für Ausländisches öffentliches Recht und Völkerrecht* 4 (1934): 261–76, 261, 270. This was of course one of the Stauffenbergs who would plot the assassination of Hitler a decade later.

142. E.g., among many, Gerhard Röhrborn, "Der Autoritäre Staat" (diss., Jena, 1935), 53; Adalbert Karl Steichele, *Das deutsche Staatsangehörigkeitsrecht auf Grund der Verordnung über die deutsche Staatsangehörigkeit vom 5. Februar 1934* (Munich: Schweitzer, 1934), 16; Theodor Maunz, *Neue Grundlagen des Verwaltungsrechts* (Hamburg: Hanseatische Verlags-Anstalt, 1934), 10n3.

143. Robert Deisz, "Rasse und Recht," in *Nationalsozialistisches Handbuch für Recht und Gesetzgebung*, 2nd ed., ed. Hans Frank (Munich: Zentralverlag der NSDAP, 1935), 47. This article was added in the second edition.

144. See Valdis O. Lumans, *Himmler's Auxiliaries: The Volksdeutsche Mittelstelle and the German National Minorities of Europe, 1933–1945* (Chapel Hill: University of North Carolina Press, 1993), 89. If Kier was typical of the functionaries in the Volksdeutsche Mittelstelle, he belonged to a relatively accomplished intellectual group, and one with relatively little connection to the worst abuses associated with the Waffen SS. See ibid., 55–56, 58.

145. Herbert Kier, "Volk, Rasse und Staat," in *Nationalsozialistisches Handbuch für Recht und Gesetzgebung*, 1st ed., ed. Hans Frank (Munich: Zentralverlag der NSDAP, 1935), 28.

146. Edgar Saebisch, *Der Begriff der Staatsangehörigkeit* (Borna-Leipzig: Noske, 1935), 42. For the 1934 date of submission of this dissertation, see verso of the title page.

147. Martin Staemmler, *Rassenpflege im völkischen Staat* (Munich: Lehmann 1935), 49.

148. Sahm, *Die Vereinigten Staaten von Amerika*, 134. For Nazi interest in measures of "education," see Chapter 2.

149. Otto Harlander, "Französisch und Englisch im Dienste der rassenpolitischen Erziehung," *Die Neueren Sprachen* 44 (1936): 61–62. For another contemporary example

without a Nazi bent, see Josef Stulz, *Die Vereinigten Staaten von Amerika* (Freiburg im Breisgau: Herder, 1934), 314; and for more Nazi examples of the commonplace citation of American immigration law in the literature of the early 1930s, see Drascher, *Vorherrschaft der Weissen Rasse*, 370; Steichele, *Das deutsche Staatsangehörigkeitsrecht*, 14; Gottfried Neesse, *Die Nationalsozialistische Deutsche Arbeiterpartei. Versuch einer Rechtsdeutung* (Stuttgart: W. Kohlhammer, 1935), 169n19.

150. Krieger, *Rassenrecht*, 74–109.

151. Cornelia Essner, *Die "Nürnberger Gesetze" oder die Verwaltung des Rassenwahns, 1933–1945* (Paderborn: Schöningh, 2003), 82–83.

152. Kurt Daniel Stahl, "Erlösung durch Vernichtung. Von Hitler zu Nasser. Das bizarre Schicksal des deutschen Edelmannes und Professors Johann von Leers," *Die Zeit*, May 30, 2010, http://www.zeit.de/2010/22/GES-Johann-von-Leers.

153. Johann von Leers, *Blut und Rasse in der Gesetzgebung. Ein Gang durch die Völkergeschichte* (Munich: Lehmann, 1936), 80–103.

154. Saebisch, *Begriff der Staatsangehörigkeit*, 45–46.

155. Ibid., 43.

156. The Cable Act of 1922 (ch. 411, 42 Stat. 1021, "Married Women's Independent Nationality Act"), Sec. 3. Known to Germans from the discussion in Karl Zepf, "Die Staatsangehörigkeit der verheirateten Frau" (diss., Tübingen, 1929), 17–18. America was by no means the only country with a rule denaturalizing brides of foreigners, as the German literature was aware. Numerous other examples are given in Hans Georg Otto Denzer, "Die Statutenkollision beim Staatsangehörigkeitserwerb" (diss., Erlangen, 1934), 34; Alfons Wachter, "Die Staatlosen" (diss., Erlangen, 1933), 24–25. What was distinctive about the Cable Act provision was of course its race-based character.

157. Saebisch, *Begriff der Staatsangehörigkeit*, 44–45.

158. Leers, *Blut und Rasse*, 127.

159. Bernhard Lösener, "Staatsangehörigkeit und Reichsbürgerrecht," in Lammers et al., *Grundlagen, Aufbau und Wirtschaftsordnung*, 13:32.

160. Stuckart and Globke, *Kommentare*, 76.

161. Friedrich Luckwaldt, *Das Verfassungsleben in den Vereinigten Staaten von Amerika* (Berlin: Stilke, 1936), 47.

162. *Der SA-Führer* 1939, Sonderheft 10/11, 16.

163. "Wie Rassenfragen Entstehen. Weiß und Schwarz in Amerika," *Neues Volk. Blätter des Rassenpolitischen Amtes der NSDAP* 4, no. 3 (1936): 14.

164. Leers, *Blut und Rasse*, 115.

165. For the background, with a survey of differing scholarly views over the state of German public opinion at the time, see Robert Gellately, *Backing Hitler: Consent and Coercion in Nazi Germany* (Oxford: Oxford University Press, 2001), 121–24.

166. Christian Albert, "Die Staatlosen" (Niedermarsberg: Boxberger, 1933) (diss., Göttingen, 1933), 8–9: "Schwebezustand."

167. Heinrich Krieger, "Das Rassenrecht in den Vereinigten Staaten," *Verwaltungsarchiv* 39 (1934): 327.

168. Dr. L., "Das Rassenrechtsproblem in den Vereinigten Staaten," *Deutsche Justiz* 96 (September 21, 1934): 1198. This was an article summarizing Heinrich Krieger's 1934 article on the same topic for a wider Nazi audience.

169. Dietrich Zwicker, *Der amerikanische Staatsmann John C. Calhoun, ein Kämpfer gegen die "Ideen von 1789"* (Berlin: Ebering, 1935), 66, 68.

170. Ibid., 68. Zwicker did not think either deportation of the Blacks or Zionism would succeed.

171. E.g., *Deutsche Justiz* 98 (1936): 130.

172. See, e.g., the account of Grau in Chapter 2; and Adam, *Judenpolitik im Dritten Reich*, 46–64.

173. See esp. William Archibald Dunning, *Reconstruction, Political and Economic, 1865–1877* (New York: Harper, 1907), xiv: "the struggle through which the southern whites, subjugated by adversaries of their own race, thwarted the scheme which threatened permanent subjugation to another race." For the long-standing influence of the Dunning school, see Hugh Tulloch, *The Debate on the American Civil War Era* (Manchester: Manchester University Press, 1999); and for the continuing grip of the Dunning school into the 1920s and early 1930s, see Eric Foner, *Reconstruction: America's Unfinished Revolution, 1863–1877* (New York: Harper & Row, 1989), xx–xxi.

174. Krieger, "Das Rassenrecht in den Vereinigten Staaten," 329.

175. Ibid., 326–28.

176. Ibid., 330–31.

177. Sahm, *Die Vereinigten Staaten von Amerika*, 80 and generally 78–80.

178. Ibid., 95 and generally 92–96.

179. Leers, *Blut und Rasse*, 87–88.

180. Hitler, *Mein Kampf*, 490 (= Hitler, *Mein Kampf. Eine kritische Edition*, 2:1117.)

181. Sahm, *Die Vereinigten Staaten von Amerika*, 97, and the material further in 97–99. Sahm did not expressly refer to the parallels with the Nuremberg Laws, but they are inescapably present in the historical circumstances of 1936. His reference to Puerto Ricans reflects the fact that their citizenship status had changed in 1917. See Christina Duffy Burnett and Burke Marshall, "Between the Foreign and the Domestic: The Doctrine of Territorial Incorporation, Invented and Reinvented," in *Foreign in a Domestic Sense: Puerto Rico, American Expansion and the Constitution*, ed. Christina Duffy Burnett and Burke Marshall (Durham, NC: Duke University Press, 2001), 17.

182. Sahm, *Die Vereinigten Staaten von Amerika*, 98–100, again without specific reference to the Nuremberg Laws, which were however obviously in the background for any juristic dissertation on this topic.

183. Ibid., 98–99.

184. Ibid., 98–100, again without specific reference to the Nuremberg Laws.

185. Drascher, *Vorherrschaft der Weissen Rasse*, 213.

186. Krieger, *Rassenrecht*, 307.

187. Charles Vibbert, "La génération présente aux États-Unis," *Revue des Deux Mondes* 58 (1930): 329–45, 332.

188. Bertram Schrieke, *Alien Americans: A Study of Race Relations* (New York: Viking, 1936), 125.

189. Gunnar Myrdal, *An American Dilemma: The Negro Problem and Modern Democracy* (New York: Harper, 1944), 1:458.

190. Krieger, *Rassenrecht*, 305.

191. Saebisch, *Begriff der Staatsangehörigkeit*, 45–46.

192. Ibid., 46 (American immigration legislation had begun to fill what the author saw as numerous gaps in American race legislation).

193. Fitzgerald and Cook-Martin, *Culling the Masses*, 7.

CHAPTER 2: PROTECTING NAZI BLOOD AND NAZI HONOR

1. E.g., Claus Eichen, *Rassenwahn. Briefe über die Rassenfrage* (Paris: Éditions du Carrefour, 1936).

2. Gerhard Werle, *Justiz-Strafrecht und polizeiliche Verbrechensbekämpfung im Dritten Reich* (Berlin: De Gruyter, 1989), 179.

3. Entscheidungen des Reichsgerichts in Strafsachen 72, 91, 96 (Decision of 23.2.1938): "eines der Grundgesetze des nationalsozialistischen Staates"; also in *Deutsche Justiz* 100 (1938): 422–24.

4. Gustav Klemens Schmelzeisen, *Das Recht im nationalsozialistischen Weltbild. Grundzüge des deutschen Rechts*, 3rd ed. (Leipzig: Kohlhammer, 1936), 84.

5. Wilhelm Stuckart and Hans Globke, *Kommentare zur deutschen Rassengesetzgebung* (Berlin: Beck, 1936), 1:15.

6. Matthias Schmoeckel, "Helmut Nicolai," in *Neue Deutsche Nationalbiographie* 19 (Berlin: Duncker & Humblot, 1999), 205; see also Klaus Marxen, *Der Kampf gegen das liberal Strafrecht. Eine Studie zum Antiliberalismus in der Strafrechtswissenschaft der zwanziger und dreißiger Jahre* (Berlin: Duncker & Humblot, 1975), 90–91.

7. For the work of Gercke, see Cornelia Essner, *Die "Nürnberger Gesetze" oder die Verwaltung des Rassenwahns, 1933–1945* (Paderborn: Schöningh, 2003), 76–82; Alexandra Przyrembel, *"Rassenschande". Reinheitsmythos und Vernichtungslegitimation im Nationalsozialismus* (Göttingen: Vandenhoeck & Ruprecht, 2003), 103 and 103n112.

8. See Bernd-Ulrich Hergemöller, *Mann für Mann. Biographisches Lexikon zur Geschichte von Freundesliebe und Mann-Männlicher Sexualität im Deutschen Sprachraum* (Hamburg: Männerschwarmskript, 1998), 275, 536–37; and for Nicolai's arrest in the Black Forest, confession, and subsequent marriage, see Martyn Housden, *Helmut Nicolai and Nazi Ideology* (Houndmills: Macmillan, 1992), 111.

9. Przyrembel, *"Rassenschande"*; Cornelia Essner, "Die Alchemie des Rassenbegriffs," *Jahrbuch des Zentrums für Antisemitismusforschung* 4 (1995): 201–25.

10. For "education and enlightenment" as goals of Nazi policy, see below, text at Notes 75 and 86.

11. Przyrembel, *"Rassenschande,"* 104.

12. Helmut Nicolai, *Die Rassengesetzliche Rechtslehre. Grundzüge einer nationalsozialistischen Rechtsphilosophie* (Munich: Eher, 1932), 27.

13. Ibid., 45–46. For Alfred Rosenberg's 1930 linking of the two questions of citizenship and miscegenation, see Essner, *"Nürnberger Gesetze,"* 56; and for Hitler, ibid., 58.

14. Arno Arlt, "Die Ehehindernisse des BGB in ihrer geschichtlichen Entwicklung und im Hinblick auf künftige Gestaltung" (diss., Jena, 1935) (submitted December 15, 1934), 87.

15. Heinrich Krieger, *Das Rassenrecht in den Vereinigten Staaten* (Berlin: Junker & Dünnhaupt, 1936), 311: "die von Negern oft verübte Notzucht an weißen Frauen." American courts in the South could still endorse the same view two decades later. See *McQuirter v. State,* 36 Ala. App. 707, 63 So. 3d 388 (1953).

16. *Pace & Cox v. State,* 69 Alabama Rep. 231, 232 (1882), translated, quoted, and discussed in Detlef Sahm, *Die Vereinigten Staaten von Amerika und das Problem der nationalen Einheit* (Berlin: Buchholz & Weisswange, 1936), 68.

17. Cited and discussed in David Bernstein, *Rehabilitating Lochner: Defending Individual Rights against Progressive Reform* (Chicago: University of Chicago Press, 2011), 80–81.

18. Bilbo quoted and discussed in Ira Katznelson, *Fear Itself: The New Deal and the Origins of Our Time* (New York: Liveright, 2013), 86.

19. E.g., Philippa Levine, "Anthropology, Colonialism and Eugenics," in *Oxford Handbook of the History of Eugenics,* ed. Alison Bashford and Philippa Levine (New York: Oxford University Press, 2010), 52–54.

20. Transcript of Meeting of Strafrechtskommission, June 5, 1934, in Jürgen Regge and Werner Schubert, eds., *Quellen zur Reform des Straf- und Strafprozeßrechts* (Berlin: De Gruyter, 1989), 2:2, pt. 2:277.

21. Richard Espenschied, *Rassenhygienische Eheverbote und Ehebeschränkungen aus allen Völkern und Zeiten* (Stuttgart: Olnhausen & Warth, 1937), 52–54, surveying the law in the United States; and 57 noting that prohibitions are elsewhere left to the church.

22. For the prohibition on bigamy in German criminal law under the Reichsstrafgesetzbuch of 1871, see Reichsstrafgesetzbuch § 171. There were certainly earlier precedents for criminalization of forms of marriage other than bigamy, but the Nazis did not to my knowledge make use of them. The Theodosian Code included a criminalization of religiously mixed marriage targeting Jews. See Amnon Linder, *The Jews in Roman Imperial Legislation* (Detroit: Wayne State University Press, 1987), 178–82, for texts and commentary; and medieval examples are traced, e.g., for Iberia by David Nirenberg, *Communities of Violence: Persecution of Minorities in the Middle Ages* (Princeton: Princeton University Press, 1996), 129–38. Other forms of plural marriage were of course also in principle subject to prosecution in Western Europe, but were too rare to figure prominently in the discussions leading up to the Nuremberg Laws.

23. The Northern Territory Aboriginal Act 1910 (SA) (Austl.), s. 22.

24. For the broader legislative landscape and context, and the conclusion that Australian legislation looked "mild by comparison" to American, see Katherine Ellinghaus, *Taking Assimilation to Heart: Marriages of White Women and Indigenous*

Men in the United States and Australia, 1887–1937 (Lincoln: University of Nebraska Press, 2006), 202–3; and for the limited consequences of agitation in New Zealand, see Angela Wanhalla, *Matters of the Heart: A History of Interracial Marriage in New Zealand* (Auckland: Auckland University Press, 2013), 134–38. For the observation that South Africa in particular lacked anti-miscegenation legislation, see Johann von Leers, *Blut und Rasse in der Gesetzgebung. Ein Gang durch die Völkergeschichte* (Munich: Lehmann, 1936), 113.

25. Md. Code Ann., Crimes and Punishments, art. 27, §§ 393, 398 (1957).

26. E.g., Espenschied, *Rassenhygienische Eheverbote*, 61, noting earlier civil invalidity in some cases; Leers, *Blut und Rasse*, 115. For the scattered foreign examples of marriage invalidity that the Nazis were able to find, see Andreas Rethmeier, *"Nürnberger Rassegesetze" und Entrechtung der Juden im Zivilrecht* (New York: Lang, 1995), 140–41n171.

27. See Essner, *"Nürnberger Gesetze,"* 136.

28. Eduard Meyer, *Die Vereinigten Staaten von Amerika. Geschichte, Kultur, Verfassung und Politik* (Frankfurt: Keller, 1920), 93–94: "Unmasse."

29. Lothar Gruchmann, *Justiz im Dritten Reich, 1933–1940. Anpassung und Unterwerfung in der Ära Gürtner*, 3rd ed. (Munich: Oldenbourg, 2001), 865; cf. Gürtner in Regge and Schubert, *Quellen*, 303 (East Asia); Lösener in ibid., 306 (South America and East Asia); Gürtner in ibid., 308 (South Asia).

30. Peter Longerich, *Holocaust: The Nazi Persecution and Murder of the Jews* (Oxford: Oxford University Press, 2010), 36, 54–57, and the more circumstantial account in Longerich, *Politik der Vernichtung. Eine Gesamtdarstellung der nationalsozialistischen Judenverfolgung* (Munich: Piper, 1998), 65–115.

31. Otto Dov Kulka, "Die Nürnberger Rassengesetze und die deutsche Bevölkerung im Lichte geheimer NS-Lage- und Stimmungsberichte," *Vierteljahrshefte für Zeitgeschichte* 32 (1984): 608; Gruchmann's account in accessible article form in "'Blutschutzgesetz' und Justiz," *Vierteljahrshefte für Zeitgeschichte* 31, no. 3 (1983): 418–42, 426; Essner, *"Nürnberger Gesetze,"* 110.

32. Krieger, *Rassenrecht*, 311 ("Lynchjustiz . . . auch bei uns in ihren typischen Einzelheiten bekannt geworden ist"). While Krieger does not specifically mention pogrom violence against Jews, the phrase "auch bei uns . . . bekannt geworden" could hardly refer to anything else.

33. E.g., Longerich, *Politik der Vernichtung*, 97–98; Gruchmann, "'Blutschutzgesetz' und Justiz," 428–30.

34. Gunnar Myrdal, *An American Dilemma: The Negro Problem and Modern Democracy* (New York: Harper, 1944), 1:458.

35. Longerich, *Holocaust*, 58–59; Essner, *"Nürnberger Gesetze,"* 109–12; Uwe Dietrich Adam, *Judenpolitik im Dritten Reich* (Düsseldorf: Droste, 1972), 115, 120–24.

36. Adam, *Judenpolitik*, 115, 120–24.

37. Gruchmann, *Justiz im Dritten Reich*, 864.

38. Essner, *"Nürnberger Gesetze,"* 96; and for the political context, see Longerich, *Politik der Vernichtung*, 84–95.

39. For its importance and radical character, see Gruchmann, *Justiz im Dritten Reich*, 764–71. It was to be sure not an official party document, but the work of radicals pushing a program that was not at first realized. See Marxen, *Der Kampf gegen das liberal Strafrecht*, 120.

40. Helmut Ortner, *Der Hinrichter: Roland Freisler, Mörder im Dienste Hitlers* (Darmstadt: Wissenschaftliche Buchgesellschaft, 1993).

41. See Gruchmann, *Justiz im Dritten Reich*, 760.

42. Ibid., 764–65.

43. Abundant details on the relevant legal debates are given in Rethmeier, "*Nürnberger Rassegesetze*," 55–69. Dissolving existing marriages was difficult, since no obvious legal grounds existed. Nazi theorists tried to deal with this difficulty by holding that the passage of Nazi legislation had made the importance of race membership clear, so that Aryan spouses could contest their marriages on the grounds that they had been mistaken as to the nature of the union. See ibid., 56–57.

44. Hanns Kerrl, ed., *Nationalsozialistisches Strafrecht. Denkschrift des Preußischen Justizministers* (Berlin: Decker, 1933), 47–49 (hereinafter *Preußische Denkschrift*).

45. Grau, in Regge and Schubert, *Quellen*, 279: "sehr eingeschränkt."

46. *Preußische Denkschrift*, 49. I have reproduced the full text of this section of the *Preußische Denkschrift* at http://press.princeton.edu/titles/10925.html.

47. See Gruchmann, *Justiz im Dritten Reich*, 770–71, on Freisler's gratification at seeing the program of the Denkschrift triumph.

48. E.g., Karl Dietrich Bracher, *The German Dictatorship: The Origins, Structure, and Effects of National Socialism*, trans. Jean Steinberg (New York: Praeger, 1970), 238–40; Norbert Frei, *National Socialist Rule in Germany: The Führer State, 1933–1945*, trans. Simon B. Steyne (Oxford: Blackwell, 1993), 23–27; Ian Kershaw, *Hitler, 1889–1936: Hubris* (New York: Norton, 1999), 470–71. Of course it is the case that some Germans regarded the Night of the Long Knives as a triumph for order. See, e.g., ibid., 517. Nevertheless there was no mistaking its significance for the collapse of traditional ideas of legality.

49. Gruchmann, *Justiz im Dritten Reich*, 868, repeating his judgment in his earlier article, observes that Gürtner's objections were based on "Überlegungen rechtlicher und—wie bei Männern wir Gürtner angenommen werden kann—ethischer Art."

50. On a careful assessment of the evidence, Gruchmann concludes that Gürtner probably did not act improperly to favor Hitler in the Beer Hall Putsch proceedings. See Gruchmann, *Justiz im Dritten Reich*, 34–48.

51. Ibid., 79. For Gürtner's enduring commitment, if conditional, to the Rechtsstaat, see ibid., 68–78; and for his non-anti-Semitism, see ibid., 71. For the assessment of Gürtner as a "genuine conservative" working "to retain the last vestiges of a legal order," see Elisabeth Sifton and Fritz Stern, *No Ordinary Men: Dietrich Bonhoeffer and Hans von Dohnanyi, Resisters against Hitler in Church and State* (New York: NYRB Books, 2013), 45.

52. Claudia Koonz, *The Nazi Conscience* (Cambridge, MA: Harvard University Press, 2003), 171–77.

53. Cf. Freisler's concessions in Regge and Schubert, *Quellen*, 285, 286; and, e.g., Arlt, "Ehehindernisse des BGB."

54. See Rethmeier, *"Nürnberger Rassegesetze,"* 54–69.

55. For the general background, see Rethmeier, *"Nürnberger Gesetze"*, 70–82.

56. Cf. Lawrence Friedman, "Crimes of Mobility," *Stanford Law Review* 43 (1991): 637–58, 638: "The bigamist and the swindler both committed what might be called crimes of identity. Their crimes turned on false pretenses, on disguised personality, on lies about one's past." It is important to observe that earlier forms of bigamy involved more collusion between the two parties. See Sara A. McDougall, *Bigamy and Christian Identity in Late Medieval Champagne* (Philadelphia: University of Pennsylvania Press, 2012).

57. Gesetz zur Bekämpfung der Geschlechtskrankheiten, February 18, 1927, Reichsgesetzblatt (1927), 1:61, § 6; cf. Klee in Regge and Schubert, *Quellen*, 290; Freisler in Regge and Schubert, *Quellen*, 338; *Preußische Denkschrift*, 50.

58. This was Dohnanyi, in Regge and Schubert, *Quellen*, 325–26, making the striking argument that criminalizing only "malicious deception" was conceptually incoherent, since the interest such a criminalization protected was that of the individual, and not, as the *Denkschrift* demanded, of the race.

59. Essner, *"Nürnberger Gesetze,"* 83.

60. See below, "Defining 'Mongrels': The One-Drop Rule and the Limits of American Influence."

61. This is the ultimate judgment of Essner, despite her hostility toward Lösener. Essner, *"Nürnberger Gesetze,"* 173.

62. For a brief recent biography, see Hans Christian Jasch, *Staatssekretär Wilhelm Stuckart und die Judenpolitik* (Munich: Oldenbourg, 2012), 481, and further details of Lösener's doings in the immediate aftermath of the war in ibid., 396–97. Lösener's biography is subjected to an important skeptical treatment in Essner, *"Nürnberger Gesetze,"* 113–34. An English translation of some of the relevant material is in Karl Scheunes, ed., *Legislating the Holocaust: The Bernhard Lösener Memoirs and Supporting Documents*, trans. Carol Scherer (Boulder, CO: Westview, 2001).

63. Adam, *Judenpolitik*, 135–37; Essner, *"Nürnberger Gesetze,"* 160–61.

64. See below, text at Note 166.

65. The distinctive feature of the 1691 Virginia statute, unlike its 1664 Maryland predecessor, was that it barred relations with nonwhites "bond or free," no longer limiting itself to master–slave relations. See Peggy Pascoe, *What Comes Naturally: Miscegenation Law and the Making of Race in America* (Oxford: Oxford University Press, 2009), 19–20. Lying in the background here is an issue of considerable importance that I cannot discuss in this book: the shift from a social-status-based conception of hierarchy to a race-based conception. See Benedict Anderson, *Imagined Communities: Reflections on the Origins and Spread of Nationalism* (London: Verso, 1991), 149–50. The contrast between the Virginia statute and contemporary French law is particularly striking. The relevant provision of the 1685 Code Noir, Art. 9, far from banning miscegenation, was designed to encourage marriage "dans les formes observées par l'Église." Robert Chesnais, ed., *Le Code Noir* (Paris: L'Esprit Frappeur,

1998), 21. Only the 1724 version introduced, in Art. 6, a ban. Ibid., 43–44. For the shift from the 1685 to the 1724 code, see Peter Sahlins, *Unnaturally French: Foreign Citizens in the Old Regime and After* (Ithaca, NY: Cornell University Press, 2004), 182–83. For reference to some French legislation and decisions, and the observation that miscegenation rules were not in fact applied in practice, see Louis Charles Antoine Allemand, *Traité du Mariage et de ses Effets* (Paris: Durand, 1853), 1:129–30. Early anti-miscegenation legislation in the West focused on religiously mixed marriages, not racially mixed ones. See Note 22 and, e.g., Dagmar Freist, "Between Conscience and Coercion: Mixed Marriages, Church, Secular Authority, and Family," in *Mixed Matches: Transgressive Unions in Germany from the Reformation to the Enlightenment*, ed. David M. Luebke and Mary Lindemann (New York: Berghahn, 2014), 104–9.

66. Interest in American miscegenation legislation included the influential Geza von Hoffman's *Rassenhygiene in den Vereinigten Staaten* of 1913. See Stefan Kühl, *The Nazi connection: Eugenics, American Racism, and German National Socialism* (New York: Oxford University Press, 1994),16.

67. Mont. Code Ann., ch. 49 §§ 1–4 (1909); S.D. Civil Code, ch. 196 § 1 (1909); N.D. Cent. Code., ch. 164, § 1 (1909); Wyo. Stat. Ann., ch. 57, § 1 (1913).

68. Jens-Uwe Guettel, *German Expansionism, Imperial Liberalism, and the United States, 1776–1945* (Cambridge: Cambridge University Press, 2012), 127–60. The enthusiasm for America led Germans into error at least once. Franz-Josef Schulte-Althoff, "Rassenmischung im kolonialien System. Zur deutschen Rassenpolitik im letzten Jahrzehnt vor dem Ersten Weltkrieg," *Historisches Jahrbuch* 105 (1985): 64, describes German admiration for the anti-miscegenationist views of the "American" Bishop Montgomery. Montgomery was, however, British. The remarks that enthused Germans can be found in *The Pan-Anglican Congress, 1908: Special Report of Proceedings &c., Reprinted from The Times* (London: Wright, 1908), 122. For the larger political setting and history, see Dieter Gosewinkel, *Einbürgern und Ausschließen. Die Nationalisierung der Staatsangehörigkeit vom Deutschen Bund bis zur Bundesrepublik Deutschland* (Göttingen: Vandenhoek & Ruprecht, 2001), 303–9.

69. Wahrhold Drascher, *Die Vorherrschaft der Weissen Rasse* (Stuttgart: Deutsche Verlags-Anstalt, 1936), 217.

70. See Birthe Kundrus, "Von Windhoek nach Nürnberg? Koloniale 'Mischehenverbote' und die nationalsozialistische Rassengesetzgebung," in *Phantasiereiche. Zur Kulturgeschichte des deutschen Kolonialismus*, ed. Birthe Kundrus (Frankfurt: Campus, 2003), 110–31.

71. For central importance of this meeting and a careful account of the debates, see Gruchmann, *Justiz im Dritten Reich*, 864–68; Przyrembel, *"Rassenschande,"* 137–43; and Essner, *"Nürnberger Gesetze,"* 99–106. See also Koonz, *Nazi Conscience*, 171–77. I have rendered "Strafrechtskommission" as "Commission for Criminal Law Reform."

72. There is a full version of the transcript, and an abbreviated version edited down in consultation with the participants. Regge and Schubert, *Quellen*, 223n1. In this book I quote from the longer version.

73. These were Grau, Klee, and Schäfer. See *Preußische Denkschrift*, 10–11.

74. See especially the careful account of Gruchmann, *Justiz im Dritten Reich*, 865–68.

75. Regge and Schubert, *Quellen*, 278; 298, 316, for other forms of deception.

76. See the assessment of Przyrembel, *"Rassenschande,"* 138; and the review of the debates over how far an approach based on "arglistige Täuschung" could extend in Essner, *"Nürnberger Gesetze,"* 103–4; alongside ibid., 151–52, for the subsequent regulatory drafting process.

77. Regge and Schubert, *Quellen*, 281–83. For Kohlrausch as a defender of the rule of law, cf. Eberhard Schmidt, *Einführung in die Geschichte der deutschen Strafrechtspflege*, 3rd ed. (Göttingen: Vandenhoeck & Ruprecht, 1965), 450–51.

78. See below, text at Note 106.

79. Dahm in Regge and Schubert, *Quellen*, 293; Freisler in Regge and Schubert, *Quellen*, 288; Klee in Regge and Schubert, *Quellen*, 290–91.

80. See the quotations from Grau below, text at Notes 84–87.

81. Regge and Schubert, *Quellen*, 288, 300.

82. Cf. Dahm on the "aktivistischen, führenden Kreisen der Studentenschaft." In Regge and Schubert, *Quellen*, 292. Gleispach also highlighted the truth of these student demands. Ibid., 295–96.

83. E.g., Regge and Schubert, *Quellen*, 283–88, here 286. Freisler was acknowledging that there must be a preliminary decision to render mixed marriages invalid—a "politische Entscheidung . . . daß dieser Grundsatz des Nationalsozialismus durchgeführt werden soll."

84. On Grau, see Ernst Klee, *Das Personenlexikon zum Dritten Reich. Wer War Was vor und nach 1945?* (Frankfurt: Fischer, 2003), 197. The text quoted is included among leading documents in the Nazi persecution of the Jews in Götz Aly et al., eds., *Die Verfolgung und Ermordung der europäischen Juden durch das nationalsozialistische Deutschland* (Munich: Oldenbourg, 2008), 1:346–49.

85. Regge and Schubert, *Quellen*, 280. Freisler held that the proposed criminalization of "Verletzung der Rassenehre" could be salvaged by dropping the express reference to "colored races." Ibid., 287, 308–309. Elsewhere he defended the term "colored." See below, text at Note 117.

86. Regge and Schubert, *Quellen*, 278–79.

87. Ibid., 279.

88. Klee, below, text at Note 104.

89. Regge and Schubert, *Quellen*, 280–81.

90. Ibid., 281.

91. Ibid., 281–82.

92. Sifton and Stern, *No Ordinary Men*, 46–47.

93. Ibid., 126.

94. Regge and Schubert, *Quellen*, 282.

95. Ibid., 282.

96. Ibid., 282.

97. Though perhaps he was not too far off: criminal prosecution was "sporadic." See Pascoe, *What Comes Naturally*, 135–36.

98. Regge and Schubert, *Quellen*, 282.

99. E.g., Gürtner in Regge and Schubert, *Quellen*, 307, discussing American statutes in detail.

100. On Klee, see Christian Kasseckert, *Straftheorie im dritten Reich* (Berlin: Logos, 2009), 179.

101. Regge and Schubert, *Quellen*, 315.

102. See *Brown v. Board of Education*, 347 US 483, 494 (1954).

103. See Avraham Barkai, *Vom Boykott zur "Entjudung." Der wirtschaftliche Existenzkampf der Juden im Dritten Reich* (Frankfurt: Fischer, 1987), 26–28.

104. Regge and Schubert, *Quellen*, 315.

105. For the importance of this principle in German law, and its violation by the Nazis, see Hans-Ludwig Schreiber, *Gesetz und Richter. Zur geschichtlichen Entwicklung des Satzes nullum crimen, nulla poena sine lege* (Frankfurt: Metzner, 1976).

106. Regge and Schubert, *Quellen*, 283, speaking here of illegitimate births.

107. Ibid., 306.

108. Ibid., 307.

109. Ibid., 318. Lösener here was making limited concessions to Freisler, while emphasizing education and the principle *in dubio pro reo*.

110. See Ernst Schäfer in Regge and Schubert, *Quellen*, 314 and 319; Freisler in Regge and Schubert, *Quellen*, 310, 312, 320.

111. This was Schäfer.

112. Regge and Schubert, *Quellen*, 319. Freisler declared that he had not faced this difficulty before the meeting. Ibid., 313.

113. Ibid., 319–20.

114. Ibid., 320.

115. I offer this phrase, of course, as an echo of our contemporary phrase "the social construction of race." See, e.g., Ian F. Haney López, "The Social Construction of Race: Some Observations on Illusion, Fabrication and Choice," *Harvard Civil Rights–Civil Liberties Law Review* 29 (1994): 1–62.

116. Regge and Schubert, *Quellen*, 320. For "foreign races," see the quote from Grau, above text at Note 86.

117. Ibid. Freisler had in mind the workings of the courts under the Erbhofgesetz. Regge and Schubert, *Quellen*, 309, 317, and esp. 320. Grau too looked to the Erbhofgesetz; ibid., 278. Meanwhile Schäfer defended "primitive" approaches over "scientific" ones; ibid., 314.

118. Robert Rachlin, "Roland Freisler and the Volksgerichtshof: The Court as an Instrument of Terror," in *The Law in Nazi Germany: Ideology, Opportunism, and the Perversion of Justice*, ed. Alan E. Steinweis and Robert D. Rachlin (New York: Berghahn, 2013), 63. Cf., e.g., Uwe Wesel, "Drei Todesurteile pro Tag," *Die Zeit*, February 3, 2005, http://www.zeit.de/2005/06/A-Freisler.

119. Regge and Schubert, *Quellen*, 310, 312, 320.

120. Ibid., 321; cf. ibid., 323.

121. See Essner, *"Nürnberger Gesetze,"* 102, calling him (I believe incorrectly) "Kurt."

122. Regge and Schubert, *Quellen*, 334.

123. E.g., Gürtner in ibid., 316, with detailed discussion of the Montana statute.

124. See below, text at Note 145–148.

125. Regge and Schubert, *Quellen*, 227n3.

126. Heinrich Krieger, "Principles of the Indian Law and the Act of June 18, 1934," *George Washington Law Review* 3 (1935): 279–308, 279.

127. Ibid.

128. For his thanks to Otto Koellreutter and others, see Krieger, *Rassenrecht*, 11; and for his fellowship in the Notgemeinschaft der deutschen Wissenchaft in Düsseldorf, see Krieger, "Principles of the Indian Law," 279.

129. See Heinrich Krieger, " 'Eingeborenenrecht?' Teleologische Begriffsbildung als Ausgangspunkt für die Kritik bisherigen und den Aufbau zukünftigen Rechts," *Rasse und Recht* 2 (1938): 116–30, dated at Windhoek and identifying Krieger as "Mitarbeiter des Rassenpolitischen Amtes der NSDAP."

130. Heinrich Krieger, *Das Rassenrecht in Südafrika* (Berlin: Junker & Dünnhaupt, 1944), 12. For his early African writings, see Krieger, " 'Eingeborenenrecht?' "; Heinrich Krieger, *Das Rassenrecht in Südwestafrika* (Berlin: Junker & Dünnhaupt, 1940); and for the commission from the Rassenpolitisches Amt to study South Africa, his "Vorwort" to Krieger, *Rassenrecht in Südafrika*, 11.

131. Krieger, *Rassenrecht in Südafrika*, 11, dated "Im Felde."

132. Assuming that I have identified him correctly, Krieger became Studienrat and then Oberstudienrat at the Gymnasium Philippinum zu Weilburg. He is identifiable not only because of his continuing international outlook, but also because he continued to write in a social scientific vein about the same British world he had written about in earlier years. See Heinrich Krieger, "Fakten und Erkenntnisse aus der englischen Volkszählung," *Die Neueren Sprachen* (neue Folge) 1 (1952): 87–91. For his work as an advocate of reconciliation with France and European unification: "Europa-Union Oberlahn feiert 60-Jähriges Jubiläum," http://www.oberlahn.de/29 -Nachrichten/nId,178202,Von-der-Gr%C3%BCndung-1954-1955-bis-2014.html; as a promoter of aid and student exchange in Africa and Asia: "Rund um den Pakistanberg. Völkerfreundschaft an der Lahn," *Die Zeit*, September 4, 1964, http://www .zeit.de/1964/36/rund-um-den-pakistanberg; Wolfgang Henss, "Entwicklungshilfe aus Pakistan. Volksverständigung. Vor 50 Jahren veränderten asiatische Studenten Kubach," *Weilburger Tageblatt*, August 8, 2014, http://www.mittelhessen.de/lokales /region-limburg-weilburg_artikel,-Entwicklungshilfe-aus-Pakistan-_arid,326225 .html; for his supervision of postwar exchange programs with France and England, Heinrich Krieger, "Grundsätzliche Erfahrungen aus einem internationalen Schüleraustausch," *Neuphilologische Zeitschrift* 3 (1951): 354–60; for his activity as cofounder of the Europäischer Erzieherbund: Wolfgang Mickel, *Europa durch Europas Schulen. 40 Jahre EBB/AEDE* (n.p.: Frankfurt, 1999), 2.

133. Krieger, "Principles of the Indian Law," 304, 308.

134. Quoted in Guettel, *German Expansionism*, 209—though Guettel is quite prepared to minimize the horror.

135. Heinrich Krieger, "Das Rassenrecht in den Vereinigten Staaten," *Verwaltungsarchiv* 39 (1934): 316. The original quotation appears in Thomas Jefferson, *Works*, ed. Paul Leicester Ford (New York: Putnam, 1904), 1:77.

136. Krieger, *Rassenrecht*, 49–53.

137. Ibid., 55–61.

138. Ibid., 327–49; and 57 on the "lebensfremder Positivismus" of the ideology of equality. Krieger's argument deserves a lengthier account than I can give it here. See, for example, his effort in *Rassenrecht*, 337–39, to account for the social foundations of the ideology of equality in the labor markets, and to describe the countertendency of racist sentiment to "break through."

139. For the teachings of Burgess, Dunning, and their followers, see Hugh Tulloch, *The Debate on the American Civil War Era* (Manchester: Manchester University Press, 1999), 212–20, and for the continuing grip of the Dunning school into the 1920s and early 1930s, Eric Foner, *Reconstruction: America's Unfinished Revolution, 1863–1877* (New York: Harper & Row, 1989), xx–xxi.

140. E.g., especially, among others cited in this book, Roland Freisler, "Schutz von Rasse und Erbgut im werdenden deutschen Strafrecht," *Zeitschrift der Akademie für deutsches Recht* 3 (1936): 142–46, 146, giving a list of American states with anti-miscegenation legislation, along with a description of Jim Crow segregation.

141. Krieger, "Rassenrecht," 320.

142. Krieger, *Rassenrecht*, 16.

143. The reference is to *Monroe v. Collins*, 17 Ohio St. 665 (1867).

144. Krieger, "Rassenrecht," 319–20.

145. Herbert Kier, "Volk, Rasse und Staat," in *Nationalsozialistisches Handbuch für Recht und Gesetzgebung*, 1st ed, ed. Hans Frank (Munich: Zentralverlag der NSDAP, 1935), 17–28.

146. Ibid., 26–27.

147. Arthur Gütt, Herbert Linden, and Franz Maßfeller, *Blutschutz- und Ehegesundheitsgesetz* 2nd ed., (Munich: Lehmann, 1937), 17–19. This was reprinted in turn from another republication in the *Rassenpolitische Auslands-Korrespondenz*. Ibid., 17.

148. Kier, "Volk, Rasse und Staat," 27–28. Also reproduced without attribution in Gütt, Linden, and Maßfeller, *Blutschutz- und Ehegesundheitsgesetz*, 19.

149. Kier, Volk, Rasse und Staat, 28.

150. Ibid., 28.

151. I can find few references in the non-German literature. Of the copies held in America that I have inspected, those at both Princeton and Columbia were acquired after the war, when the holdings of Nazi libraries must have been distributed to American universities. The Yale copy, by contrast, was acquired in 1935.

152. Helmut Nicolai, "Rasse und Recht," in *Deutscher Juristentag* (Berlin: Deutscher Rechts-Verlag, 1933), 1:176.

153. *Preußische Denkschrift*, 47, italics mine.

154. Konrad Zweigert and Hein Kötz, *Introduction to Comparative Law*, 3rd ed., trans. Tony Weir (New York: Oxford University Press, 1998), 16.

155. Philipp Depdolla, *Erblehre, Rasse, Bevölkerungspolitik; vornehmlich für den Unterricht in höheren Schulen bestimmt* (Berlin: Metzner, 1934), 90.

156. Otto Harlander, "Französisch und Englisch im Dienste der rassenpolitischen Erziehung," *Die Neueren Sprachen* 44 (1936): 62.

157. Essner, *"Nürnberger Gesetze,"* 77–78, 81.

158. Bill Ezzell, "Laws of Racial Identification and Racial Purity in Nazi Germany and the United States: Did Jim Crow Write the Laws That Spawned the Holocaust?," *Southern University Law Review* 30 (2002–3): 1–13; Judy Scales-Trent, "Racial Purity Laws in the United States and Nazi Germany: The Targeting Process," *Human Rights Quarterly* 23 (2001): 259–307.

159. [Anon.], "Volkstümer und Sprachwechsel," *Nation und Staat: Deutsche Zeitschrift für das europäische Minoritätenproblem* 9 (1935): 348. This journal was published in Vienna, but the article in question was reprinted without citation from some other, presumably German, source.

160. Ibid.

161. Ibid.

162. Leers, *Blut und Rasse*, 89–90.

163. The reference is to *Bell v. State*, 33 Tex. Cr. R. 163 (1894). Krieger's source here was presumably Gilbert Thomas Stephenson, *Race Distinctions in American Law* (New York: Appleton, 1910), 17: "Some states have allowed facts other than physical characteristics to be presumptive of race. Thus, it has been held in North Carolina that if one was a slave in 1865, it is to be presumed that he was a Negro. The fact that one usually associates with Negroes has been held in the same State proper evidence to go the jury tending to show that he is a Negro. If a woman's first husband was a white man, that fact, in Texas, is admissible evidence tending to show that she is a white woman."

164. *Entwurf zu einem Gesetz zur Regelung der Stellung der Juden*, in Otto Dov Kulka, ed., *Deutsches Judentum unter dem Nationalsozialismus* (Tübingen: Mohr Siebeck, 1997), 1:38; also in Aly et al., eds., *Verfolgung und Ermordung der europäischen Juden*, 1:123–24. For the association of this proposal with the moderate camp, see Essner, "Nürnberger Gesetze," 84.

165. For the drafting history of these regulations, see Essner, "Nürnberger Gesetze," 155–73; and the earlier account of Jeremy Noakes, "'Wohin gehören die "Judenmischlinge"?' Die Entstehung der ersten Durchführungsverordnung zu den Nürnberger Gesetzen," in *Das Unrechtsregime. Internationale Forschung über den Nationalsozialismus*, ed. Ursula Büttner (Hamburg: Christians, 1986), 2:69–89.

166. Text available at http://www.verfassungen.de/de/de33-45/reichsbuerger35 -v1.htm.

167. Bernhard Lösener, "Staatsangehörigkeit und Reichsbürgerrecht," in *Grundlagen, Aufbau und Wirtschaftsordnung des Nationalsozialistischen Staates*, ed. H.-H. Lammers et al. (Berlin: Spaeth & Linde, 1936), 13:32. The harder-line view of Stuckart and Globke held that it was a matter of blood, not inclination: "Durch seine *Verheiratung mit einem Juden* beweist ein Mischling ersten Grades, daß sein jüdischer Blutanteil stärker als sein deutscher Blutanteil wirkt." Stuckart and Globke, *Kommentare*, 76.

168. See Chapter 1. It is certainly the case that a woman's loss of nationality through marriage was a familiar and much-discussed possibility, which clearly influenced some Nazi thinking. See Adalbert Karl Steichele, *Das deutsche Staatsangehörigkeitsrecht auf Grund der Verordnung über die deutsche Staatsangehörigkeit vom 5.*

Februar 1934 (Munich: Schweitzer, 1934), 69. What was distinctive about the Cable Act rule was however its specifically race-based character.

NOTES TO CONCLUSION

1. Quoted in Roland Peter, "Es ging nur noch darum, wie man stirbt," *Die Zeit*, http://www.zeit.de/1990/45/es-ging-nur-noch-darum-wie-man-stirbt/komplettansicht.

2. On Fischer, "Spitzenfunktionär" in Warsaw, see Josef Wulf, *Das Dritte Reich und seine Vollstrecker. Die Liquidation von 500 000 Juden im Ghetto Warschau* (Berlin: Arani, 1961), 311–12; and, e.g., Reuben Ainsztein, *The Warsaw Ghetto Revolt* (New York: Holocaust Library, 1979), 3, 105. Fischer is now mostly unremembered, but his work in the early 1930s has made its way into one recent standard text. See Ludwig Fischer, "Rasseschande als strafbare Handlung (1935)," in *Rechtfertigungen des Unrechts. Das Rechtsdenken im Nationalsozialismus in Originaltexten*, ed. Herlinde Pauer-Studer and Julian Fink (Berlin: Suhrkamp, 2014), 411–15.

3. In January 1933, a dollar cost 4.2 reichsmarks; by January 1934 it had fallen to 2.61, and by January 1935 to 2.48. See the tables in http://www.history.ucsb.edu /faculty/marcuse/projects/currency.htm.

4. "Herbst-Studienfahrt des BNSDJ. nach Nordamerika," *Deutsches Recht* 5 (1935): 379.

5. See "Studienfahrt des BNSDJ. nach den Vereinigten Staaten von Nordamerika," *Wirtschaftstreuhänder* 14/15 (1935): 344.

6. "Studienfahrt des BNSDJ. nach Nordamerika," *Deutsche Justiz* 97 (1935): 1424, col. 2.

7. "Brodsky Releases 5 in Bremen Riot," *New York Times*, September 7, 1935, 1, 5.

8. "Hotel Is Picketed as Nazis Depart," *New York Times*, September 28, 1935, L13.

9. Ibid.

10. Ibid.

11. See http://www.dailymail.co.uk/news/article-2296911/Amon-Goeth-Did-executed -Nazi-murderer-Schindlers-List-escape-justice.html. The New York City Bar Association preserves no record of their visit, unfortunately.

12. Johnpeter Horst Grill and Robert L. Jenkins, "The Nazis and the American South in the 1930s: A Mirror Image?," *Journal of Southern History* 58, no. 4 (November 1992): 667–94; George Fredrickson, *Racism: A Short History* (Princeton: Princeton University Press, 2002), 2, 129.

13. See Ariela J. Gross, *What Blood Won't Tell: A History of Race on Trial in America* (Cambridge, MA: Harvard University Press, 2008), 5–7.

14. See, e.g., Bertram Schrieke, *Alien Americans: A Study of Race Relations* (New York: Viking, 1936).

15. Edgar Saebisch, *Der Begriff der Staatsangehörigkeit* (Borna-Leipzig: Noske, 1935), 42.

16. David Scott Fitzgerald and David Cook-Martin, *Culling the Masses: The Democratic Origins of Racist Immigration Policy in the Americas* (Cambridge, MA: Harvard University Press, 2014), 7.

17. Fitzgerald and Cook-Martin, *Culling the Masses*, 260, discussing Vargas's importation of the US national origins model.

18. Marilyn Lake and Henry Reynolds, *Drawing the Global Colour Line: White Men's Countries and the International Challenge of Racial Equality* (Cambridge: Cambridge University Press, 2008), 29, 35, 49–74 (influence of Bryce), 80, 119, 129–31, 138–44, 225, 269. Lake and Reynolds also note American admiration for Australia at, e.g., 313; there was certainly a larger sense of shared white mission. Nevertheless the prominence of the American example, as represented by figures like Bryce and others they survey, shines out in their study.

19. Jens-Uwe Guettel, *German Expansionism, Imperial Liberalism, and the United States, 1776–1945* (Cambridge: Cambridge University Press, 2012), 127–60.

20. Their main example, as Andreas Rethmeier, *"Nürnberger Rassegesetze" und Entrechtung der Juden im Zivilrecht* (New York: Lang, 1995), 140, notes, was the South African criminalization of interracial extramarital sex. See, e.g., Rolf Peter, "Bevölkerungspolitik, Erb- und Rassenpflege in der Gesetzgebung des Dritten Reiches," *Deutsches Recht* 7 (1937): 238n1. The extramarital sex issue deserves more attention than I can give to it in this book.

21. Hanns Kerrl, ed., *Nationalsozialistisches Strafrecht. Denkschrift des Preußischen Justizministers* (Berlin: Decker, 1933), 47.

22. There is lively disagreement over this question, beginning with the treatment of *limpieza de sangre* in sixteenth-century Iberia. For conflicting views, see Henry Kamen, *The Spanish Inquisition: A Historical Revision* (London: Weidenfeld and Nicholson, 1997), 239–41; and María Elena Martinez, *Genealogical Fictions: Limpieza de Sangre, Religion, and Gender in Colonial Mexico* (Stanford: Stanford University Press, 2008), 45. It is manifestly the case that there is a history of the sources of American racism to be sought in the Iberian tradition. See James H. Sweet, "The Iberian Roots of American Racist Thought," *William and Mary Quarterly* 54 (1997): 143–66.

23. See Fitzgerald and Cook-Martin, *Culling the Masses*, 261.

24. Johann von Leers, *Blut und Rasse in der Gesetzgebung. Ein Gang durch die Völkergeschichte* (Munich: Lehmann, 1936).

25. Lake and Reynolds, *Drawing the Global Colour Line*.

26. See Chapter 1.

27. See James Q. Whitman, "From Fascist 'Honour' to European 'Dignity,'" in *Darker Legacies of Law in Europe: The Shadow of National Socialism and Fascism over Europe and its Legal Traditions*, ed. C. Joerges and N. Ghaleigh (Oxford: Hart, 2003), 243–66; Whitman, "'Human Dignity' in Europe and the United States: The Social Foundations," *Human Rights Law Journal* 25 (2004): 17–23.

28. Daniel Howe, *What Hath God Wrought: The Transformation of America, 1815–1848* (Oxford: Oxford University Press, 2007), 37. Cf., e.g., Anthony Marx, *Faith in Nation: Exclusionary Origins of Nationalism* (New York: Oxford University Press, 2003), ix–x.

29. Hitler, *Mein Kampf*, 143–44 ed. (Munich: Eher, 1935), 479 (= Hitler, *Mein Kampf. Eine kritische Edition*, eds. Christian Hartmann, Thomas Vordermayer, Othmar Plöckinger, and Roman Töppel [Munich: Institut für Zeitgeschichte, 2016], 2:1093–95).

30. Cf. Jochen Thies, *Architekt der Weltherrschaft: Die "Endziele" Hitlers* (Düsseldorf: Droste, 1976), 41–45.

31. Theodore Roosevelt, "National Life and Character," in *American Ideals and Other Essays Social and Political* (New York: Putnam, 1897), 289. Quoted and discussed in Lake and Reynolds, *Drawing the Global Colour Line*, 102.

32. For a famous Nazi-era discussion, see Carl Schmitt, *Völkerrechtliche Grossraumordnung*, 3rd ed. (Berlin: Deutscher Rechtsverlag, 1941), 19–20.

33. See Chapter 1.

34. The much-discussed exception is *Buchanan v. Warley*, 245 US 60 (1917).

35. Desmond King and Rogers Smith, "Racial Orders in American Political Development," *American Political Science Review* 99 (2005): 75–92.

36. Gunnar Myrdal, *An American Dilemma: The Negro Problem and Modern Democracy* (New York: Harper, 1944), 1:458.

37. Ira Katznelson, *Fear Itself: The New Deal and the Origins of Our Time* (New York: Liveright, 2013).

38. See ibid., 166, and the figures compiled at http://law2.umkc.edu/faculty/projects /ftrials/shipp/lynchingyear.html.

39. Albrecht Wirth, *Völkische Weltgeschichte (1879–1933)* (Braunschweig: Westermann, 1934), 10.

40. Waldemar Hartmann, "Deutschland und die USA. Wege zu gegenseitigem Verstehen," *Nationalsozialistische Monatshefte* 4 (November 1933): 493–94.

41. Ralf Michaels, "Comparative Law by the Numbers," *American Journal of Comparative Law* 57 (2009): 765–95, 769.

42. Hermann Mangoldt, review of Karl Llewellyn, *Präjudizienrecht und Rechtsprechung in Amerika*, *Archiv für Rechts- und Sozialphilosophie* 27 (1933): 304. It is worth observing that Mangoldt, later to become a leading commentator on postwar German constitutional law, was another figure who began his career, when a Nazi, as a student of American law. See his *Rechtsstaatsgedanke und Regierungsform in den Vereinigten Staaten von Amerika* (n.p. [Essen]: Essener Verlagsanstalt, 1938).

43. Paul Mahoney, "The Common Law and Economic Growth: Hayek Might Be Right," *Journal of Legal Studies* 30 (2001): 504–5. In response to a comment from an anonymous reader, I should emphasize that I do not mean to imply that professional legal historians or legal philosophers concern themselves with the views of Hayek. My aim is to capture a more general attitude toward the common law.

44. See esp. the seminal account in Edward Glaeser and Andrei Shleifer, "Legal Origins," *Quarterly Journal of Economics* 107 (2002): 1193–1229.

45. H.L.A. Hart, "Positivism and the Separation of Law and Morals," *Harvard Law Review* 71 (1958): 617.

46. Lon Fuller, "Positivism and Fidelity to Law—A Reply to Professor Hart," *Harvard Law Review* 71 (1958): 633. The Hart/Fuller debate has done much to distort Anglo-American understanding.

47. See especially the fundamental work of Bernd Rüthers, *Die unbegrenzte Ausle-gung. Zum Wandel der Privatrechtsordnung im Nationalsozialismus*, 7th ed. (Tübingen: Mohr Siebeck, 2012).

48. "Der Eid auf Adolf Hitler," in Rudolf Hess, *Reden* (Munich: Zentralverlag der NSDAP, 1938), 12.

49. Ian Kershaw, "Working towards the Führer," *Contemporary European History* 2 (1993): 103–18, 116–17. This book is not the place to enter into the larger debate about functionalism versus intentionalism on the road to the Holocaust, nor about the precise nature of Hitler's role, since I do not make any effort to assess relevant evidence. I cite the material in the text purely for its importance in judging the legal historical questions that the book raises.

50. See classically C. C. Langdell, "Harvard Celebration Speeches," *Law Quarterly Review* 3 (1887): 124.

51. Laurence Tribe, *American Constitutional Law* (New York: Foundation, 2000), 1:14.

52. Cf. Stefan Kühl, *The Nazi Connection: Eugenics, American Racism, and German National Socialism* (New York: Oxford University Press, 1994), 15: "European eugeni-cists admired the success of their American counterparts in influencing eugenics legislation."

53. The centrality of the Nazi commitment to lawlessness is now emphasized in Anselm Döring-Manteuffel, "Gesetzesbruch als Prinzip. Entwicklungslinien des Weltanschaulichen Radikalismus in der Führerdiktatur," *Zeitschrift der Savigny-Stiftung für Rechtsgeschichte (Germanistische Abteilung)* 132 (2015): 420–40.

54. See the discussion of Freisler's views in Cornelius Broichmann, *Der außeror-dentliche Einspruch im Dritten Reich* (Berlin: Erich Schmidt Verlag, 2014), 163; and the sensitive assessment of Ralph Angermund, "Die geprellten 'Richterkönige'. Zum Niedergang der Justiz im NS-Staat," in *Herrschaftsalltag im Dritten Reich*, ed. Hans Mommsen and Susanne Willems (Düsseldorf: Schwann, 1988), 304–73, 320–21.

55. Broichmann, *Der außerordentliche Einspruch*, 168–71; cf. *Preußische Denkschrift*, 115–16.

56. For a discussion placing the law of the era in its larger intellectual context, see the classic account of Holmes in Morton White, *Social Thought in America: The Revolt against Formalism* (New York: Viking, 1949), 59–75.

57. See Marcus Curtis, "Realism Revisited: Reaffirming the Centrality of the New Deal in Realist Jurisprudence," *Yale Journal of Law and Humanities* 27 (2015): 157–200.

58. Brian Leiter, "American Legal Realism," in *Guide to the Philosophy of Law and Legal Theory*, ed. Martin Golding and William Edmundson (Oxford: Blackwell, 2005), 50.

59. Address at Oglethorpe University, May 22, 1932, http://newdeal.feri.org/speeches /1932d.htm.

60. Jack M. Balkin, "Wrong the Day It Was Decided," *Boston University Law Re-view* 85 (2005): 677–725, 686.

61. Friedrich Luckwaldt, *Das Verfassungsleben in den Vereinigten Staaten von Amer-ika* (Berlin: Stilke, 1936), 51.

62. This is not the place to discuss these figures, but Americans should know about the most striking example, Theodor Maunz, who became the leading commentator on German constitutional law after World War II. After his death it was revealed that throughout his career, Maunz had contributed anonymous articles to a far-right-wing newspaper. See http://www.zeit.de/1994/07/maunz-raus. It seems that this man, the embodiment of the liberal constitutionalism of the Federal Republic, never abandoned his Nazi sympathies.

63. Morton Horwitz, *The Transformation of American Law, 1879–1960: The Crisis of Legal Orthodoxy* (New York: Oxford University Press, 1992), 188.

64. Joachim Rückert, "Der Rechtsbegriff der deutschen Rechtsgeschichte in der NS-Zeit: der Sieg des 'Lebens' und des konkreten Ordnungsdenkens, seine Vorgeschichte und seine Nachwirkungen," in *Die deutsche Rechtsgeschichte in der NS-Zeit*, ed. Rückert (Tübingen: Mohr Siebeck, 1995), 177; cf., e.g., Gerhard Werle, *Justiz-Strafrecht und polizeiliche Verbrechensbekämpfung im Dritten Reich* (Berlin: De Gruyter, 1989), 144–45. For a statement from a leading German legal thinker, emphasizing both the continuities with Weimar jurisprudence and the importance of according authority to judges, see Philipp Heck, *Rechtserneuerung und juristische Methodenlehre* (Tübingen: Mohr Siebeck, 1936), 5–6.

65. Wolfgang Greeske, *Der Gedanke der Verfassung in der neueren Staatslehre* (Saalfeld: Günther, n.d.), 109. For the earlier history of this theme, see now Katharina Schmidt, "Law, Modernity, Crisis: German Free Lawyers, American Legal Realists, and the Transatlantic Turn to 'Life,' 1903–1933," *German Studies Review* 39, no. 1 (2016): 121–40.

66. G. Edward White, "From Sociological Jurisprudence to Realism: Jurisprudence and Social Change in Early Twentieth-Century America," in *Patterns of American Legal Thought* (Indianapolis: Bobbs-Merrill, 1978), 140.

67. I quoted and discussed this letter in James Q. Whitman, "Commercial Law and the American Volk: A Note on Llewellyn's German Sources for the Uniform Commercial Code," *Yale Law Journal* 97 (1987): 156–75, 170; and it was also quoted and discussed in N.E.H. Hull, *Roscoe Pound and Karl Llewellyn: Searching for an American Jurisprudence* (Chicago: University of Chicago Press, 1997), 237. The University of Chicago informs me that it is no longer to be found among Llewellyn's papers. I issue here a plea to any scholar who may have inadvertently removed it to return it. My own notes have long since vanished, so that I cannot be certain which Nazi comment on Llewellyn was meant, but I assume that it was Mangoldt's review, cited in Note 40.

68. William Scheuerman, *Morgenthau* (Cambridge: Polity, 2009), 25.

69. Nor of course does it mean that the New Deal held interest only for fascists. There were plenty of European progressives who saw things to admire in it. See Daniel Rodgers, *Atlantic Crossings: Social Politics in a Progressive Age* (Cambridge, MA: Harvard University Press, 1998), 410–11 and generally 409–84 for the transatlantic connections.

70. See James Q. Whitman, "The Case for Penal Modernism," *Critical Analysis of Law* 1 (2014): 143–98.

71. See, e.g., Kevin McMahon, *Reconsidering Roosevelt on Race: How the Presidency Paved the Road to Brown* (Chicago: University of Chicago Press, 2004), 12 and passim.

72. I cite only the appalling Blutschutzgesetz decision, Entscheidungen des Reichsgerichts in Strafsachen 72, 91, 96 (Decision of February 23, 1938). The spirit of gleeful lawlessness in such decisions is unmatched in the United States, I think. Others may differ.

73. See Jamal Greene, "The Anticanon," *Harvard Law Review* 125 (2011): 438–39.

74. See the controversial claims of David Bernstein, *Rehabilitating Lochner: Defending Individual Rights against Progressive Reform* (Chicago: University of Chicago Press, 2011), 73–89; cf. Note, "Legal Realism and the Race Question: Some Realism about Realism on Race Relations," *Harvard Law Review* 108 (1995): 1607. The bulk of this Note traces the undoubted opposition to racist law of some leading realists, including Llewellyn, Hale, and Felix Cohen, but the author is also obliged to note that "the majority of canonical Realists avoided the race question." Ibid., 1619. For the larger intellectual context, see Thomas C. Leonard, *Illiberal Reformers: Race, Eugenics and American Economics in the Progressive Era* (Princeton: Princeton University Press, 2016), 109–28.

75. Heinrich Krieger, *Das Rassenrecht in den Vereinigten Staaten* (Berlin: Junker & Dünnhaupt, 1936), 327–49; and 57 on the "lebensfremder Positivismus" of the ideology of equality. Guettel, *German Expansionism*, 200–201, misreads Krieger's book on this score, interpreting him as far more of a critic of the United States than is the case, and than he was understood to be in Nazi Germany. See, e.g., Schmidt-Klevenow, review of Krieger, *Das Rassenrecht in den vereinigten Staaten, Juristische Wochenschrift* 111 (1936): 2524, praising Krieger's account of an "uns deutschen innerlich nahestehenden Landes."

76. Karl J. Arndt, review of Krieger, *Das Rassenrecht in den Vereinigten Staaten, Books Abroad* 12 (1938): 337–38.

77. For parallels between Nazi criminal justice and criminal justice in contemporary America, see James Q. Whitman, *Harsh Justice: Criminal Punishment and the Widening Divide between America and Europe* (New York: Oxford University Press, 2003), 202–3. Long-term confinement for habitual offenders was one of the antiliberal measures demanded by the Prussian Memorandum, *Preußische Denkschrift*, 138—though also calling for systematic treatment for alcoholics, the mentally ill, and others. This book is not the place to discuss the complexities of Nazi punishment practices.

78. See esp. William J. Stuntz, "The Pathological Politics of Criminal Law," *Michigan Law Review* 100 (2001–2): 505–600.

79. I have made this argument more fully in Whitman, *Harsh Justice*, 199–203.

SUGGESTIONS FOR
FURTHER READING

The is no such thing as an uncontroversial list of suggested readings about Nazi Germany. Nevertheless, few would disagree that Ian Kershaw's writings make an ideal starting point for English-speaking readers who wish to delve deeper. For the period discussed in this book, his *Hitler, 1889–1936: Hubris* (New York: Norton, 1999) is a model of readable scholarship, founded on careful judgments and intimate knowledge of the sources, events, and debates. For an extensive English-language chronicle of the events surrounding the emergence of the Nuremberg Laws, readers can turn to Peter Longerich, *Holocaust: The Nazi Persecution and Murder of the Jews* (Oxford: Oxford University Press, 2010).

Nazi interest in American law should be seen against the larger background of European fascination with, and sometimes revulsion toward, American culture. Victoria de Grazia, *Irresistible Empire: America's Advance through Twentieth-Century Europe* (Cambridge, MA: Harvard University Press, 2005) is a masterful account. David Ellwood's *The Shock of America: Europe and the Challenge of the Century* (New York: Oxford University Press, 2012), is a wide-ranging study, focusing on European responses to American culture and economy in the wake of America's rise to the status of preeminent global power, while Adam Tooze's *The Deluge: The Great War, America and the Remaking of the Global Order, 1916–1931* (New York: Penguin, 2014), is a probing exploration of foreign relations. The intellectual cross-currents of the first decades of the twentieth century are the subject of Daniel Rodgers's indispensable and illuminating study *Atlantic Crossings: Social Politics in a Progressive Age* (Cambridge, MA: Harvard University Press, 1998).

Most of the literature on American influence abroad has revolved around American popular culture, American consumerism, and the industrial innovations of Henry Ford and Frederick Winslow Taylor. In recent years, though, historians have taken a growing interest in the place of American race policies and eugenics on the world stage. Marilyn Lake and Henry Reynolds, *Drawing the Global Colour Line: White Men's Countries and the International Challenge of Racial Equality* (Cambridge: Cambridge University Press, 2008), is an excellent study, focusing on the Anglophone world. Race-based immigration law in particular is the subject of David Scott Fitzgerald and David Cook-Martin, *Culling the Masses: The Democratic Origins of Racist Immigration Policy in the Americas* (Cambridge, MA: Harvard University Press, 2014). These books make it clear that America was not just a cultural and economic icon, but also an international beacon of race-conscious policy in the late nineteenth and early twentieth centuries.

As for the American influence on Germany in particular, Stefan Kühl's *The Nazi Connection: Eugenics, American Racism, and German National Socialism* (New York: Oxford University Press, 1994) remains a fundamental text on the Nazi engagement with American eugenics. The German fascination with the American conquest of the West has been recounted by a number of German historians. For a vigorous argument and citations to further literature, see Carroll P. Kakel, *The American West and the Nazi East: a Comparative and Interpretive Perspective* (New York: Palgrave Macmillan, 2011). For other aspects of the German attitude toward America, there is insightful and challenging work in the essays of Philipp Gassert and Detlef Junker in *Transatlantic Images and Perceptions: Germany and America since 1776*, ed. David E. Barclay and Elisabeth Glaser-Schmidt

(New York: Cambridge University Press, 1997) and in Mary Nolan, *Visions of Modernity: American Business and the Modernization of Germany* (New York: Oxford University Press, 1994). Jens-Uwe Guettel, *German Expansionism, Imperial Liberalism, and the United States, 1776–1945* (Cambridge: Cambridge University Press, 2012), includes valuable research on pre-Nazi periods but is in my view unreliable on the Nazi period itself.

The parallels between Nazi race policies and Jim Crow America are discussed in two important studies: Johnpeter Horst Grill and Robert L. Jenkins, "The Nazis and the American South in the 1930s: A Mirror Image?," *Journal of Southern History* 58, no. 4 (November 1992): 667–94, and George Fredrickson, *Racism: A Short History* (Princeton: Princeton University Press, 2002). Grill and Jenkins make an effort to assess the extent of southern support for Hitler. Stephen H. Norwood, *The Third Reich in the Ivory Tower* (Cambridge and New York: Cambridge University Press, 2009), tracks down Nazi support among American intellectual leaders.

Some of the toughest questions raised by the research in this book involve the interpretation of the New Deal, and of American movements such as Progressivism and Legal Realism. How exactly should we see the United States of the 1920s and early 1930s in relation to the ugly regimes that emerged in Central and Southern Europe? John P. Diggins, *Mussolini and Fascism: The View from America* (Princeton: Princeton University Press, 1972), was a pioneering study of one uncomfortable issue: early New Deal Americans took a considerable interest in the models offered by the government of Fascist Italy. My own contribution on the same topic appears in James Q. Whitman, "Of Corporatism, Fascism and the First New Deal," *American Journal of Comparative Law* 39 (1991): 747–78. The parallels between New Deal and Nazi styles of government and approaches to the Great Depression are treated in John Garraty, "The New Deal, National Socialism, and the Great Depression,"

American Historical Review 78 (1973): 907–44, and Wolfgang Schi-velbusch, *Three New Deals: Reflections on Roosevelt's America, Musso-lini's Italy, and Hitler's Germany, 1933–1939*, trans. Jefferson Chase (New York: Metropolitan, 2006). None of these studies should be taken to discredit the New Deal. No serious scholar would call the United States of the early 1930s fascist. Nevertheless it seems fair to say that the scholarship has shown that there were parallels between America and Europe that raise questions to which it is not easy to give fully satisfying answers.

Further tough questions have been raised by Ira Katznelson, in two controversial books that highlight the political alliance between New Deal reformers and the racists of the Southern Democratic Party: *Fear Itself: The New Deal and the Origins of Our Time* (New York: Liveright, 2013), and *When Affirmative Action Was White: An Untold History of Racial Inequality in Twentieth-Century America* (New York: Norton, 2005). Meanwhile a number of historians have insisted on the importance of "scientific racism" and eugenics in the Progressive Era and the early New Deal. The starting point for discussion of the appeal of eugenics for leading American legal thinkers is Justice Holmes's opinion in *Buck v. Bell*, 274 US 200 (1927), with its notorious declaration that "three generations of imbeciles are enough." There is much material in the vivid and revealing study by Victoria Nourse, *In Reckless Hands: Skinner v. Oklahoma and the Near Triumph of American Eugenics* (New York: Norton, 2008). David Bernstein's controversial *Rehabilitating Lochner: Defending Individual Rights against Progressive Reform* (Chicago: University of Chicago Press, 2011), makes a case for the dark side of Progressivism in the law, while Thomas C. Leonard, *Illiberal Reformers: Race, Eugenics and American Economics in the Progressive Era* (Princeton: Princeton University Press, 2016), looks at economics.

All of these works paint a darker picture of early twentieth-century American intellectual and political life than we might wish. So does this book.

INDEX